Elegant Comfort Food

from the

DORSET INN

Elegant Comfort Food
from the
DORSET INN

JANE & MICHAEL STERN

RUTLEDGE HILL PRESS
Nashville, Tennessee
A Division of Thomas Nelson Publishers
Since 1798

www.thomasnelson.com

Published by Rutledge Hill Press, a Division of Thomas Nelson, Inc., P.O.
Box 141000, Nashville, Tennessee, 37214.

Rutledge Hill Press books may be purchased in bulk for educational, business, fundraising, or sales promotional use. For information, please email
SpecialMarkets@ThomasNelson.com.

Library of Congress Cataloging-in-Publication Data

Stern, Jane.
    Elegant comfort food from the Dorset Inn / Jane & Michael Stern.
      p. cm.
Includes index.
    ISBN 1-4016-0198-7 (hardcover)
    1. Cookery. I. Stern, Michael, 1946— II. Dorset Inn. III. Title.
    TX714.S771 2005
    641.5—dc22

                                    2005009606

Printed in the United States of America

05 06 07 08 09-5 4 3 2 1

To the wonderful spirit
of my sister "smebs"
Deborah P. Axelrod

CONTENTS

ACKNOWLEDGMENTS

The Dorset Inn had been a town landmark for a few centuries when we came across it some three years ago. We were dazzled: first by breakfast, then by dinner, then by a few more meals that seemed to us the epitome of elegant Yankee comfort food. Then, when we got to know the place itself and Sissy Hicks and her wonderful staff and adorable dogs, we were convinced that here was exactly the sort of restaurant we yearn to discover . . . and love to write about. So, when we say that putting together a book about this place was a pleasure, we mean it. We loved every minute, whether hanging around the inn for leisurely breakfasts or trying out the excellent recipes at home. We are so grateful to Sissy for her willingness to contribute whatever was needed all along the way. She is what hospitality is all about.

We thank Rutledge Hill Press for having made a reality of our dream of commemorating favorite restaurants around the country in a series of Roadfood cookbooks. In particular, we are grateful to Pamela Clements, Roger Waynick, and Larry Stone, who have shared our passion for great meals around the country, and whose support and belief in this series make it happen. We also thank Geoff Stone for his scrupulous editing and Bryan Curtis for his good ideas to spread the word.

The friendship and guidance of our comrades at *Gourmet* magazine are a constant inspiration as we travel around the country researching our "Roadfood" column. Like many writers, we tend to write with particular readers in mind—readers who motivate us to do our best. In this case, Ruth Reichl, James Rodewald, and "Doc" Willoughby are muses who are always at our side.

We never hit the road without our virtual companions at Roadfood.com—Steve Rushmore Sr., Stephen Rushmore and Kristin Little, Cindy Keuchle, and Marc Bruno—who constantly fan the flames of appetite and discovery along America's highways and byways. As the Web site has grown, we have found ourselves part of a great national community of people who love to travel and explore local foodways as much as we do. For the support and

encouragement of all those who take part in the ongoing adventure of Roadfood.com, we are deeply obliged.

Thanks also to agent Doe Coover for her tireless work on our behalf, and to Jean Wagner, Jackie Willing, Mary Ann Rudolph and Ned Schankman for making it possible for us to travel in confidence that all's well at home.

FOREWORD

Quite simply, I love food. I have had a wonderful journey these last thirty plus years being able to devote my time, as well as my passion, to the preparation and serving of a vast variety of food. My focus has evolved to an emphasis on mostly organic and locally grown products. I have become dedicated to supporting dairy farmers, farmers markets, bread makers, etc.

Loyal customers, both local and those who come to stay at my inn, have helped to create a terrific restaurant. The atmosphere has remained casual with an emphasis on quality and consistency, and I am fortunate to have a great staff that knows and interacts with everyone. Breakfast is my favorite meal, both to cook and to eat! My cuisine is often described as "comfort food," most likely because I really do cook from my heart and try to stay away from "trendy" dishes.

Most recently, I have become involved in the Slow Food movement, which has greatly enhanced my philosophies in the kitchen. The mission of Slow Food is to support artisans who grow, produce, market, and prepare wholesome foods. The movement also supports the revival of the kitchen and the table as centers of pleasure, culture, and economy. I am most grateful to Misse and Chris as inspirations for the induction of the Slow Food movement into my cuisine.

It is a joy to be able to share my recipes with you, and my hope is that you have as much pleasure in preparing them as I have had. There is so much that goes into the development of the interpretations of food, and I am incredibly lucky to have been surrounded by some wonderful sous-chefs and interns throughout the years. They have each given more than they have taken away. The remaining "cogs-in-the-wheel" of my staff are also invaluable-my bartenders, front desk staff, housekeepers, landscape technicians, wait staff-their net worth is incalculable. I hope that Elegant Comfort Food from the Dorset Inn will make cooking for you a little easier, a little better, a lot more fun, and it will encourage you to seek adventure in your own kitchen.

—Sissy Hicks

INTRODUCTION

The Dorset Inn sings of Green Mountain character. Its two-century history, its setting on the village green, its broad front porch just right for rocking, its inviting hearth and broadplank floors all contribute to an enveloping sense of place that could be nowhere else. When you eat here—breakfast, lunch, or dinner—you are savoring Vermont at its very best.

Chef and owner Sissy Hicks calls the meals she makes comfort food, and they are. But like the town of Dorset itself, this is a very fine kind of country comfort with an unmistakable air of elegance. Yes, you can have meat and potatoes for supper, but the meat may be pot roast Provençale and the potatoes may be roasted reds stuffed with puréed yams. Not that there is anything ostentatious about the food service here. The dinner tables, especially in the tavern, are as cozy as a club room. While the Dorset Inn is a destination for travelers in search of good food (and traditional accommodations for the night), it is also where locals come for lunch and supper to enjoy each other's company as well as the delicious meals.

It is not easy to define the Dorset Inn's cuisine. It is categorically local in terms of ingredients, from Green Mountain maple syrup for morning waffles to small farm beefsteak and wild fiddlehead ferns at dinner. But Chef Hicks doesn't make a fetish of Vermont cuisine. "I pick up ideas here and there," she says. "I throw stuff together; I always find ways to put leftovers to good use. I cook the way it feels right. I never

ventured off into nouvelle cuisine or anything like that. My mentors are James Beard and Julia Child. Like them, my joy comes from sharing good food. If there is a theme to what I do, it is natural simplicity." While she can dazzle guests with such culinary tours-de-force as breast of chicken stuffed with brie and coriander with pear and cider sauce, her repertoire is replete with masterful renditions of such down-to-earth dinners as braised lamb shanks, corned beef and cabbage, and turkey croquettes. Her own favorite dish—and, amazingly, the most popular meal at the inn—is liver and onions. There is none better, anywhere.

Sissy didn't learn to cook when she was growing up on a dairy farm in Chester County, Pennsylvania. "I was always outside in the fields," she recalls. And when she came to Vermont for the first time in 1973, she had no intention whatsoever of going into the hospitality business. She came to ski. "I never left," she says with a broad smile. "I landed in Dorset, and I stayed." She found work as a chambermaid at the town's venerable old Barrows House under the direction of innkeepers Marilyn and Charlie Schubert. She ended up in the kitchen washing dishes. "The chef taught me how to do veggies," Sissy says. "I went from there." The kitchen was small enough that she found herself learning some of everything;

then one day, the chef left. "There I was," she remembers. "My first night solo I did 109 dinners. Marilyn and Charlie asked if I would like to continue. I said, 'Sure!'"

After five years cooking at the Barrows House, Sissy was approached by a frequent guest, New York restaurateur Joe Allen. "I like your food," he told her. "It's basic; it's simple; it's good." Allen asked Sissy to come work in his London restaurant, where he wanted her to teach the staff about fundamental American comfort food. "Here I am, five years into cooking, and I am a consultant in London!" she recalls with amazement. "But in fact, I learned so much from them. And my experience with Joe Allen really kicked off my career. After working for him, I was able to say, 'I like this, and I can do it.'" Today, Sissy likes to say, "I sleep and think food."

Allen brought Sissy back to North America to open a restaurant in Toronto. But having grown up in rural Pennsylvania and coming to feel part of the village of Dorset, she was not happy living a city life. After getting the Toronto restaurant underway, she returned to Dorset and the Barrows House. She formed a partnership with some friends in 1983 and bought it.

Vermont's oldest continuously operating inn showed its two centuries of age. It was run-down top to bottom. "We totally gutted the place," Sissy says. "Plumbing, wiring, it all had to be redone. First we did the front of the inn; that's the oldest part. We did the rooms upstairs, and we put in the bar. The one really good thing was that the old kitchen was huge. There was plenty of room. Amazingly, we still have the dishwasher that was here when we moved in, and it works like a charm. Even many of our pots and pans are original!"

As for the personality of the kitchen and the specifics of the menu, Sissy sees the reborn inn as an opportunity to continue her mission of serving comfort food that expresses the soul of the region. "I see the inn more as a home than a business," she says. "I am here every day. Whoever comes to eat is my guest. I don't want anyone to feel like they are going out to a haughty restaurant. I want them to feel they are here to dine in the home of a friend."

Breakfast

French Toast

Buttermilk Pancakes

Buckwheat Pancakes

Corn Cakes

Warm Blueberry Banana Compote

Hot Apple Oatmeal Cereal

Bran Muffins

Buttermilk Biscuits

Aunt Phinney's Granola

French Toast

Using a real French baguette gives French toast an entirely different nature than that made with ordinary sliced bread. This is French toast with character . . . and creamy insides.

6	eggs
¼	cup sugar
1	teaspoon ground cinnamon
1	teaspoon ground nutmeg
2	cups milk
	French baguette
4	tablespoons (½ stick) butter for sautéing

Preheat the oven to 400°F. Whisk the eggs, sugar, cinnamon, nutmeg, and milk in a medium bowl. Slice the baguette on the diagonal into eight ½-inch slices. Dip them in the egg mixture until thoroughly soaked. Heat the butter in a medium sauté pan over medium-high heat. When the butter is hot but not burnt, add the bread slices. Brown on one side then turn and brown the other side. Transfer to a baking dish and bake until golden brown and fluffy, about 8 minutes.

MAKES 4 SERVINGS, 2 SLICES PER PERSON

Buttermilk Pancakes

Our favorite memory of eating pancakes at the Dorset Inn is sitting in the sunny breakfast room and watching Sissy's late bassett hound, Fergie, saunter up to our table and plaintively look up in hopes of getting a snack. Who could resist? We gave Fergie her pancake without maple syrup, but for human consumption, syrup is a must!

2	cups all-purpose flour
2	teaspoons baking powder
1	teaspoon baking soda
2	tablespoons sugar
1	teaspoon vanilla extract
¼	teaspoon ground nutmeg
½	teaspoon salt
2	eggs
2	cups buttermilk

In a large mixing bowl combine the flour, baking powder, baking soda, sugar, vanilla, nutmeg, and salt. Whisk together the eggs and the buttermilk in a separate bowl. Slowly whisk the egg mixture into the flour mixture. That's it! Drop small dollops of the pancake batter on a lightly buttered griddle or pan over medium heat. Brown the pancakes on both sides.

MAKES 4 SERVINGS

Buckwheat Pancakes

The tawny character of buckwheat cakes gets a delicious tang from the buttermilk in this batter. For some reason buckwheat pancakes seem more right when they have a smaller diameter.

1	cup buckwheat flour
1	cup all-purpose flour
2	teaspoons baking powder
1	teaspoon baking soda
½	teaspoon salt
2	eggs
2	cups buttermilk

Mix the flours, baking powder, baking soda, and salt together in a medium bowl. In a small bowl, whisk together the eggs and buttermilk. Slowly whisk the egg mixture into the flour mixture. Drop small dollops of the pancake batter on a lightly buttered and heated pan or griddle. Brown the pancakes on both sides.

MAKES 4 SERVINGS

Corn Cakes

Corn cakes are a favorite New England variation on the theme, and they are especially wonderful if you have fresh, sweet kernels just cut off the cob. If you do, save some of that "milk" that comes away when you cut them and add it to the batter for flavor.

2	cups yellow cornmeal
1	cup flour
2	tablespoons sugar
2	teaspoons baking powder
2	teaspoons baking soda
1	teaspoon salt
4	eggs
2	cups buttermilk
2	cups fresh or frozen (and thawed) corn kernels

Mix the cornmeal, flour, sugar, baking powder, baking soda, and salt together in a medium bowl. In a separate bowl, whisk together the eggs and the buttermilk. Gently whisk the egg mixture into the flour mixture. Fold in the corn. Drop the batter onto a well-buttered griddle or pan over medium heat. Brown on both sides.

MAKES 6 SERVINGS

BREAKFAST IN VERMONT

Vermont is a great place to eat breakfast. It is blessed with smokehouses that
make superior sausage, ham, and bacon,
as well as with countless bakeries where
the repertoires range from serious cake
donuts to featherweight croissants.
Early-to-rise farmhouse hours plus a
high wholegrain consciousness plus the
legendary maple syrup harvest equal

superior stacks of flapjacks. Consider also the custom of turning yester-
day's boiled dinner leftovers into savory corned beef hash, and the North
Country's abundance of short-order diners, charming B&Bs, and vintage
country inns. For appetites on dawn patrol, the prospects are boundless.

Breakfast in the Dorset Inn's garden room is our vision of morning
in heaven. Irregularly shaped buttermilk pancakes come studded with
brilliant blueberries; crunchy, raised waffles have the old-style, small
tread surface that holds countless droplets of swirled melting butter and
maple syrup; and the corned beef hash is a patty with an outside crunch
that surrounds a glistening center of ragged, brick-red beef shreds,
nuggets of carrot, and caramel-brown ribbons of onion.

When we first came across the Dorset Inn one evening, a sign outside read "Lunch and Dinner." But as we had our first wonderful meal
in the tavern, Nuni, the head waitress, explained that "yes, breakfast is
served too; the sign-painter just didn't have room to include all three
meals!" Since then, a new sign has been posted listing breakfast; and
while many of the morning people in the dining room are overnight
guests of the inn, locals and travelers consider Sissy Hicks' place a destination for a truly home-style way to start the day.

Sissy does everything herself in the mornings, plate by plate. And
when she has the opportunity between cooking people's meals, she'll
pull out "Big Orange," the rudimentary orange juicer she bought at
K-Mart twenty years ago for a few dollars. "I've tried all the high-tech
commercial juicers," she says as she squeezes fresh juice from oranges,
half-by-half. "But I always come back to Big Orange."

Warm Blueberry Banana Compote

A luxurious topping for French toast or pancakes . . . or even for ice cream at dessert. Be sure to serve it warm.

2	*cups fresh blueberries, washed, or frozen blueberries, thawed*
2	*bananas, sliced*
½	*cup honey*
1	*teaspoon ground cinnamon*

Preheat the oven to 350°F. Combine the blueberries, bananas, honey, and cinnamon in a small roasting pan. Bake for 30 minutes, stirring occasionally. The blueberries and bananas will be soft. Serve at once or refrigerate for later use.

MAKES 6 TO 8 SERVINGS

Hot Apple Oatmeal Cereal

It's amazing just how wonderful real oatmeal tastes if you've grown accustomed to the quick-cook kind. Sissy's version, sweetened with brown sugar, apples, and raisins is a hearty, healthy meal.

4	cups milk
½	cup brown sugar
2	tablespoons butter
½	teaspoon salt
½	teaspoon ground cinnamon
2	cups rolled oats
2	cups chopped apple
1	cup raisins

Preheat the oven to 350°F. Mix the milk, brown sugar, butter, salt, and cinnamon in a heavy, ovenproof pot and bring to a boil. Immediately remove from the heat and add the oats, apple, and raisins. Return the pot to the heat and bring to a simmer. Then put the pot in the oven, covered, and bake for 30 minutes.

MAKES 4 TO 6 SERVINGS

Bran Muffins

Every region of the country has its own favorite morning breadstuff, including cinnamon rolls in Iowa, biscuits throughout the South, and buttered Cuban toast in Tampa. In New England, donuts are big, but muffins are even more beloved. Muffin making is an art from Connecticut to the Canadian border. Sissy's bran muffins have a rugged texture that make them a joy to tear into hunks along with that morning cup of coffee.

2	cups raisins
5	teaspoons baking soda
2	cups boiling water
1	cup vegetable oil
1	cup brown sugar
1	cup molasses
4	eggs
5	plus ½ cups flour
1	teaspoon salt
6	cups bran cereal
1	quart buttermilk
1	cup chopped walnuts

Combine the raisins and baking soda in a large bowl. Pour the boiling water over the raisins. Let cool. In a large bowl, mix the oil, brown sugar, and molasses. Add the eggs and beat well. Add 5 cups flour, the salt, and cereal. Pour in the buttermilk and mix together until blended. Stir in the cooled raisin mixture. Dredge the nuts in the remaining ½ cup flour and then fold them into the batter. Store in the refrigerator for 6 to 8 hours or overnight.

When ready to bake, preheat the oven to 375°F. Scoop the batter into greased muffin tins about three-quarters full and bake for 25 to 30 minutes.

MAKES 24 MUFFINS

Buttermilk Biscuits

At the Yankee table, biscuits aren't just for breakfast. The same fluffy rounds that go so well with bacon and eggs in the morning are used as the basis for traditional strawberry short-cake. They're not at all sweet, but good berries will make up for that.

4	cups all-purpose flour
1	teaspoon baking soda
5	teaspoons baking powder
1	teaspoon salt
⅔	cup butter
1 ½	cups buttermilk

Preheat the oven to 450°F. Mix together the flour, baking soda, baking powder, and salt. Cut the butter into the flour mixture with a pastry cutter or with your hands. Add the buttermilk and mix until moistened. Roll the dough out into a rectangle about ½-inch thick on a generously floured board. Cut the dough into rounds with a juice glass or biscuit cutter. Place on a baking sheet lined with parchment paper and bake in the oven for 8 to 10 minutes.

MAKES 24 BISCUITS

Aunt Phinney's Granola

Aunt Phinney is Sissy's eighty-three-year-old aunt who lives on a farm in Pennsylvania and still does everything from scratch: her own lard, meat, chickens, eggs. "She is my mentor," Sissy says. "She is the salt of the earth. She *is* slow food. She enjoys doing what she does and she has a family that enjoys eating." Aunt Phinney's granola has been a big hit among breakfasters at the Dorset Inn.

8	cups rolled oats, not instant
1¼	cups firmly packed brown sugar
1½	cups unprocessed bran
1½	cups wheat germ
¾	cup chopped walnuts
½	cup raw sunflower seeds
¾	cup honey
2	teaspoons vanilla extract
4	tablespoons ground cinnamon
½	cup vegetable oil
1	cup unsweetened coconut flakes
2	cups raisins
2	cups diced dried apricots
2	cups dried cherries

Preheat the oven to 225°F. In a large bowl combine the oats, brown sugar, bran, wheat germ, walnuts, and sunflower seeds and mix well. In a small saucepan heat the honey, vanilla, cinnamon, and oil over medium heat until bubbly, stirring constantly. Pour the hot honey mixture over the dry mixture and mix well. Spread the mixture in a large roasting pan and bake for 30 to 40 minutes, stirring well every 10 minutes. Remove from the oven and, when cool, stir in the coconut, raisins, apricots, and cherries.

MAKES 20 (1-CUP) SERVINGS

Appetizers

Smoked Trout Mousse

Chicken Liver and Sun-dried Tomato Pâte

Sautéed Oysters with Balsamic Vinaigrette

Fried Calamari with Mediterranean Salsa and Pesto

Yam Fritters

Asparagus and Fiddlehead Vinaigrette

Warm Goat Cheese and Spinach Appetizer

Sun-Dried Tomato Melbas

Cheese Ball

Steamed Mussels

Salmon Tartare

Gorgonzola Cheesecake

Smoked Trout Mousse

One of the best places to enjoy the hospitality of the Dorset Inn is the tavern around the corner from the dining room. It's a cozy place where a selection from the wine cellar or microbrew beer list goes so well with this zesty hors d'oeuvre.

4	*fillets smoked trout, boned and skinned*
2	*teaspoons lemon juice*
4	*sprigs parsley, leaves only*
1	*teaspoon horseradish*
1	*shallot*
¼	*teaspoon Dijon mustard*
1	*cup heavy cream, whipped*
	Salt and pepper

Purée the trout, lemon juice, parsley, horseradish, shallots, and mustard, in a food processor. With a rubber spatula scrape the mixture into a mixing bowl. Gently fold in the whipped cream. Add salt and pepper to taste. Chill until ready to serve.

MAKES 6 SERVINGS

Chicken Liver and Sun-Dried Tomato Pâte

Liver is earthy. Tomatoes are sunny. Combine the two with a rainbow of herbs and a good shot of brandy and you have the makings of a delicious pâte.

1	pound butter, diced, plus 4 tablespoons
½	medium onion, chopped
2	garlic cloves, chopped
2	sprigs parsley
½	teaspoon dried thyme
½	teaspoon dried sage
1	teaspoon dried tarragon
1	pound chicken livers, rinsed and cleaned
½	cup brandy (any inexpensive brandy will do)
	Salt and pepper
1	tablespoon sun-dried tomatoes, minced
½	cup clarified butter
	Melba toast or baguette of French bread, thinly sliced and toasted
	Cornichons and chopped red onion

Melt 4 tablespoons butter in a 10-inch skillet over medium heat for 2 minutes. Sauté the onion, garlic, parsley, thyme, sage, and tarragon. Add the chicken livers and cook for 5 minutes, stirring occasionally. Add the brandy and ignite—be careful, it will flame up—shaking the pan until the liquid has evaporated and the flame has gone out. Season with the salt and pepper to taste. Blend the mixture in a food processor until smooth. Gradually add the remaining 1 pound butter while the machine is running. When the mixture is well-blended, add the sun-dried tomatoes and pulse quickly, incorporating the small bits of tomato. Put into small ramekins. Serve with Melba toasts, cornishons, and red onion. Seal the ramekins with the melted clarified butter.

MAKES 12 SERVINGS

Note: To seal the ramekins with the clarified butter, chill the pâte for 30 minutes and then spoon clarified butter on top. Cover with plastic wrap and store in the refrigerator for up to four days. Bring the pâte to room temperature 30 minutes before serving.

Sautéed Oysters with Balsamic Vinaigrette

One of the few things that can improve the taste of a good, freshly-shucked oyster is a mignonette sauce. These sautéed oysters get a similar boost—and turn meltingly lush—from a quick turn in butter with balsamic vinegar.

36	oysters, shucked (Ask the fishmonger for shucked oysters, medium "Queen Selects.")	
½	cup all-purpose flour	
	Salt and pepper	
24	tablespoons (3 sticks) butter, divided	

Balsamic Vinaigrette

1	egg yolk
2	shallots
2	garlic cloves
⅓	cup balsamic vinegar
1	sprig parsley
1½	cups oil
	Salt and pepper

Lightly dust the oysters with flour, and then salt and pepper them to taste. Melt 4 tablespoons butter in a medium-size sauté pan over medium-high heat until hot but not burnt. Sauté six oysters at a time in the butter over high heat until crisp on one side (about 2 minutes). Turn over with a small spatula and continue to sauté until just crisp. Wipe out the sauté pan with a paper towel between batches. Keep the oysters warm in a low oven or just hold them at room temperature (this process goes quickly).

Prepare the Balsamic Vinaigrette. Combine the egg yolk, shallots, garlic, vinegar, and parsley in a food processor. While the machine is running, slowly add the oil. Season with the salt and pepper to taste.

Arrange the oysters on a plate and dress lightly with the Balsamic Vinaigrette.

MAKES 6 SERVINGS

Fried Calamari with Mediterranean Salsa and Pesto

I had a CIA graduate, Greg Rems, working for me a couple of years," Sissy recalls. "He got me into doing the calamari. It is crisp and tender, and the seasoning I use gives it a Mediterranean flavor. People say it is the best they've ever had."

5	cups all-purpose flour	2	tablespoons garlic powder
1	cup panko (Japanese breadcrumbs)	2	tablespoons Old Bay Seasoning
		2	pounds squid tubes and tentacles*
2	tablespoons sea salt	1	cup milk
1	tablespoon black pepper		Sprigs of fresh thyme and rosemary
2	tablespoons dried oregano		
2	tablespoons dried basil	4	cups canola oil
1	tablespoon paprika		Mediterranean Salsa (recipe follows)
1	tablespoon commercial blackening seasoning		Pesto (recipe follows)

In a large bowl combine the flour, panko, salt, pepper, oregano, basil, paprika, blackening seasoning, garlic powder, and Old Bay Seasoning and mix well. (This can be put in containers and stored.) Slice the squid tubes into rings, and put them into a bowl with the tentacles and cover with milk. Let them sit for up to 2 hours. (Sissy adds a few sprigs of fresh thyme and rosemary.) Pour the canola oil into a heavy 2-quart saucepan and heat over medium heat until the oil reaches 350°F. Toss a small amount of calamari at a time in a small amount of the crumb mixture, and carefully drop the calamari into the hot oil. Fry until golden brown. Serve with the Mediterranean Salsa and drizzle pesto around the outside of each plate.

MAKES 6 SERVINGS

*Note: Visit your local seafood market and ask for squid tubes and tentacles. Clean the tubes by inserting your finger and pulling out the spine. Sometimes they come already cleaned.

Mediterranean Salsa

6	fresh plum tomatoes, diced	2	teaspoons dried oregano
1	small red onion, finely diced	2	teaspoons balsamic vinegar
2	teaspoons minced garlic	1	tablespoon olive oil
¼	cup diced kalamata olives	1	tablespoon lemon juice
¼	cup capers		Salt and pepper
1	tablespoon minced fresh basil		

In a medium bowl combine the tomatoes, onion, garlic, olives, capers, basil, oregano, vinegar, oil, lemon juice, and salt and pepper to taste and mix well.

MAKES ABOUT 4 CUPS

Pesto

3   cups fresh basil leaves, packed

2   garlic cloves

2   tablespoons chopped parsley

2   tablespoons pine nuts

1   teaspoon salt

½   cup olive oil

½   cup finely grated Asiago or Parmesan cheese

Purée the basil, garlic, parsley, pine nuts, and salt in a food processor. Slowly add the oil while the machine is running. At the last minute, add the cheese and just pulse quickly. Store in an airtight container in the refrigerator.

MAKES ABOUT 2 CUPS

Yam Fritters

Fritters are a fine hors d'oeuvre, side dish, or snack, combining the starchy sweetness of the yam with the opulence of the fry kettle and the sparkle of their maple syrup garnish.

2	pounds yams (approximately 4 large yams)
1	tablespoon all-purpose flour plus 1 cup for dredging
½	teaspoon baking powder
½	teaspoon salt
½	teaspoon ground nutmeg
½	teaspoon ground cinnamon
1	egg, beaten
	Oil for frying
	Maple syrup

Put the yams in a medium pot and cover with water. Bring to a boil over high heat, and then reduce to a simmer. Simmer the yams until they just start to soften but are still somewhat firm. Remove from the heat. Pour off the water and cover the yams with ice to stop the cooking process and to chill quickly. Peel and grate the chilled yams with a medium grater into a large mixing bowl.

Preheat the oil in a fryer or heavy skillet to 350°F.

In a separate bowl, combine the flour, baking powder, salt, nutmeg, cinnamon, and egg and mix together thoroughly. Add the mixture to the grated yams. You should have a mixture that is a soft cookie-dough texture. Form the yam mixture into golf-ball-size balls and roll in the flour mixture. Gently deep-fry the balls in the oil for 5 minutes or until brown. Serve with the maple syrup.

MAKES 6 SERVINGS

Asparagus and Fiddlehead Vinaigrette

Spring is fiddlehead season in New England. For a very short while in late April and into May these spiral ferns (named because they resemble a violin) grow wild and abundant.

½	pound asparagus, trimmed and peeled		4	sprigs parsley
6	cups water		1	shallot
1	teaspoon salt		1	teaspoon dry mustard
½	pound fresh fiddleheads, trimmed and washed		1½	cups olive oil
				Salt and pepper

Raspberry Vinaigrette

¼	cup raspberry vinegar		Minced red onion for garnish
⅛	cup dry sherry (Dry Sak, for example)		Bacon bits for garnish
			Chopped hard-boiled egg for garnish

Steam the asparagus until al dente, about 3 minutes. Place in an ice-water bath until cool. Bring the water to a boil; add the salt and drop in the fiddleheads. Simmer until just cooked through, about 8 minutes. (Fiddleheads are a lot tastier if cooked all the way through.) Remove them from the water and place in an ice-water bath until cool. Drain the asparagus and fiddleheads and pat dry with paper towels.

Prepare the Raspberry Vinaigrette. Combine the raspberry vinegar, sherry, parsley, shallot, and mustard in a food processor. While the machine is running, slowly add the olive oil. Add salt and pepper to taste.

Arrange the asparagus and fiddleheads on a plate and drizzle with the Raspberry Vinaigrette. Garnish with the red onion, bacon bits, and hard-boiled egg.

MAKES 4 SERVINGS

Warm Goat Cheese and Spinach Appetizer

Vermont is best-known for its cheddar, but the chèvre Sissy gets for this warm hors d'oeuvre is local, too. It comes from a certified organic dairy named Does' Leap, in East Fairfield. There Kristan Doolan and George VanVlaanderen graze goats and make chèvre, feta, and Does' Leap Tomme, aged for up to six months.

2	*(8-ounce) logs goat cheese or chèvre*
1	*garlic clove*
½	*cup basil leaves*
1	*shallot*
½	*cup olive oil*
	Fine breadcrumbs
2	*pounds spinach*
	Butter
	Basil Vinaigrette (see page 74)
	Sun-Dried Tomato Melbas (see next page)

Cut the goat cheese into ¼-inch rounds with a thin knife dipped into hot water (approximately 6 slices in a log). Combine the garlic, basil, and shallot in the work bowl of a food processor. While pulsing, add the oil. Pour the mixture into a flat container and add the goat cheese rounds to marinate for 1 hour. Remove the goat cheese from the marinade. Very carefully roll the cheese slices in the breadcrumbs. Refrigerate until ready to use. Just before serving, place the rounds in a small roasting pan and heat in a 350°F oven for about 8 minutes or until soft to the touch. While the goat cheese is warming, wilt the spinach (one good handful per person) in a hot sauté pan with a little bit of butter. Just flash in and out. Arrange the spinach on six small plates. Place two pieces of goat cheese on each plate, and drizzle a bit of the Basil Vinaigrette over the top. Serve with Sun-Dried Tomato Melbas.

MAKES 6 SERVINGS

Sun-Dried Tomato Melbas

This is a wonderful way to give ordinary boxed crackers an extraordinary homemade flavor.

½   cup sun-dried tomatoes, rehydrated

1   tablespoon balsamic vinegar

2   basil leaves

½   garlic clove

½   cup olive oil

      Salt and pepper

      Melba toast

Combine the tomatoes, vinegar, basil, and garlic in a food processor. Purée until smooth. With the food processor running, slowly add the oil and salt and pepper to taste. Spread the paste on Melba toasts to serve. Serve with the Warm Goat Cheese and Spinach appetizer on page 22.

MAKES 6 SERVINGS

Cheese Ball

This recipe was inspired by a good friend of Sissy's from Maryland who suggested she try it at the inn. It turned out to be a popular appetizer, which Sissy advises can be made ahead and frozen, then defrosted at room temperature. "Garlic and good Cheddar cheese are the key," she says.

1	(8-ounce) package cream cheese
8	ounces sharp Cheddar cheese, grated
½	cup (1 stick) butter, softened
½	cup minced onion
2	garlic cloves, minced
1	teaspoon salt
¼	teaspoon cayenne
8	ounces chopped pecans
2	tablespoons diced and seeded plum tomatoes
2	tablespoons minced parsley

In an electric mixer with a paddle beat together the cream cheese, Cheddar cheese, butter, onion, garlic, salt, and cayenne until thoroughly blended. Form the mixture into a ball. Combine the pecans, tomatoes, and parsley in a bowl. Roll the cheese ball in the mixture until thoroughly coated.

MAKES 6 TO 8 SERVINGS

Steamed Mussels

Mussels are frequently served as a first course before a big lobster dinner, but whether or not lobster follows, these briny nuggets of ocean goodness are a superb way to start a meal.

4	cups white wine
1	leek, julienned
½	cup garlic butter (see page 42)
2	pounds mussels

Garlic toast

1	French baguette loaf
½	cup garlic butter

Combine the white wine, leeks, garlic butter, and mussels in a medium saucepan over medium high heat. Cover and steam for 5 to 8 minutes. The mussels will open when done; discard any that do not open. Serve in bowls with garlic toast.

For the garlic toast, simply slice the baguette and spread with garlic butter. Put on a baking sheet and place under the broiler. Watch carefully the entire time because they will brown quickly. Remove the pan and turn over the bread. Brown the other side quickly.

MAKES 6 SERVINGS

Salmon Tartare

The goodness of salmon tartar is directly dependent on the freshness and quality of the salmon used. If you are a fisherman, or know one, get your fish straight from the water and this dish will sing.

1	pound fresh salmon (Ask the fish monger to grind it, or put it in a meat grinder at home.)
1	teaspoon Dijon mustard
1	tablespoon minced capers
1	tablespoon minced shallot
2	sprigs fresh dill, minced
1	egg
½	teaspoon Worcestershire sauce
1	teaspoon lemon juice
	Melba toast or pumpernickel bread

In a small bowl combine the salmon, mustard, capers, shallot, dill, egg, Worcestershire sauce, and lemon juice and gently mix. Serve on Melba toast or pumpernickel slices. Prepare no more than 1 hour before serving to retain the freshness of the salmon.

MAKES 6 SERVINGS

Gorgonzola Cheesecake

Here is a cheesecake, served with pears, that can be dessert or hors d'oeuvre. Sissy says that she gets her excellent Gorgonzola from Boucher Farm, where it is formally labeled as Vermont Gore-dawn-zola, after Dawn, the proprietor.

32	ounces cream cheese at room temperature
4	large whole eggs
2	egg yolks
2	teaspoons all-purpose flour
6	scallions, chopped
8	ounces Gorgonzola cheese, crumbled
	Butter for greasing pan
	Breadcrumbs

Preheat the oven to 250°F. In a large mixing bowl whip the cream cheese until it is light and fluffy. Beat in the eggs and yolks one at a time. Add the flour and scallions and mix well. Mix in the Gorgonzola. Grease a 10-inch springform pan with the butter and sprinkle the bottom and sides with the breadcrumbs. Pour in the cheese mixture and bake for 1 hour until firm or a toothpick comes clean.

MAKES 12 SERVINGS

Lunch or Brunch

&

Smoked Trout Potato Pancakes

Spinach and Crab Quiche

Turkey Chili

Turkey Hash

Award-Winning Venison Chili

Scallion Pancakes

Salmon Cakes

Corned Beef Hash

Garlic Herb Corn Muffins

Mom's Corn Fritters

Garlic Mozzarella Bread

Sissy's Scones

Bacon-Potato Pancakes

Smoked Trout Potato Pancakes

This is a different brunch item that Sissy makes whenever fishermen bring her trout from nearby waters. "I love to cook trout," she says. "There is nothing better than a plate of sautéed fresh trout, scrambled eggs, and hash browns with lemon parsley better." If you can't find fresh fish, you can improvise with smoked trout.

3	large baking potatoes
2	fillets smoked trout, skinned and boned
6	slices bacon, cooked and crumbled
1	small onion, diced
1	teaspoon sea salt
½	teaspoon pepper
1	teaspoon chopped sage
½	teaspoon parsley
2	tablespoons olive oil

Cook the potatoes in a large saucepan in boiling water until they are fork tender, about 45 minutes. Cool, peel, and grate them into a large mixing bowl. Flake the trout fillets into the potatoes and add the bacon and onion. Mix in the salt, pepper, sage, and parsley. Form into six patties and refrigerate for 30 minutes to an hour. Heat the oil in a medium-size frying pan over medium heat and cook the pancakes until they are crispy and golden brown. Serve with scrambled or poached eggs.

MAKES 6 SERVINGS

Spinach and Crab Quiche

Make sure to squeeze as much moisture as possible out of the cooked spinach after parboiling it. This is a sumptuous quiche; the combination of crabmeat and cream is sheer luxury.

Dough

28	tablespoons (3½ sticks) butter, softened
½	cup milk
1	pound all-purpose flour
½	teaspoon salt

Filling

9	eggs
2	cups heavy cream
2	cups milk
2	teaspoons salt
1	teaspoon pepper
8	ounces spinach, parboiled then squeezed dry
4	ounces crabmeat
½	cup Asiago cheese

For the dough, cream together the butter and milk and add the flour and salt. Mix until a dough forms, approximately 5 minutes. Cut the dough in half, wrapping one half in plastic and freezing for later use. Let the dough rest in the refrigerator for about 1 hour. Roll out the quiche dough and fit it into a 10-inch pan, leaving approximately a ¼ to ½-inch space above the rim. Don't stretch it, but carefully press the dough into the corners of the pan, patching if needed. Freeze for half an hour.

Preheat the oven to 450°F.

For the filling, combine the eggs, cream, milk, salt, and pepper in a large mixing bowl. Purée the cooked spinach and crabmeat in a food processor. Add to the egg mixture along with the cheese and blend well. Pour the mixture into the quiche shell and bake for 15 minutes; turn the oven to 350°F and bake for 1 hour longer.

MAKES 1 (10-INCH) QUICHE OR 8 SERVINGS

VERMONT CHEESE

Vermont Cheddar is some of the best cheese in the world. Smoked with fruit wood, speckled with sage or caraway, or just plain, it is dense and extraordinarily smooth, poised between hard and moist, with a cream-rich flavor. One of the nicest ways to enjoy Vermont Cheddar is the old farmhouse way: a bowl of cold milk, a pile of biscuity store crackers and a few hunks of cheese. Crumble the crackers, break off small pieces of Cheddar into the milk, and then spoon it up!

In the early days, Vermont's culinary identity was defined by water-powered grist mills and the high-quality flour they produced for baking. The state was also known for its sheep farms, but when the market for domestic wool shrank in the mid-nineteenth century, cows became the main livestock.

Vermont's terrain is well suited for bovine grazing, and in the 1800s locals developed great dairy herds from the European breeds such as Holsteins, Jerseys, and Guernseys. Because milk spoils quickly, farmers learned to make cheese that held the milk's nutritional value in a condensed, longer-lasting form. With the introduction of refrigerated rail cars in the middle of the nineteenth century, it became possible for Vermonters to ship the cheese they made throughout the Northeast. It was coveted in Boston, Hartford, Portland, and New York. According to the Vermont Cheese Council, the state had fifty-eight factories producing cheese in 1895, and 80 percent of the state's milk went into cheese production.

You can still visit the oldest continuously operating cheese factory in our hemisphere: Crowley Cheese Factory in Healdville, just forty-five minutes northeast of Dorset, still hand-makes each batch of cheese according to an 1824 recipe, just the way it's always been done.

The Crowley Cheese Factory. Used by Permission.

Turkey Chili

Here is a recipe for red meat-frowners, in which turkey has every bit as much avoirdupois as beef. The flavor of the dish depends to a large degree on the quality of chili powder used. If you can get the real deal from the Southwest, so much the better.

4	plus 2 tablespoons vegetable oil
2	pounds ground turkey, uncooked
2	onions, diced
2	tablespoons minced garlic
½	cup chili powder
1	tablespoon cumin
2	teaspoons oregano
2	teaspoons red pepper flakes
1	teaspoon salt
2	teaspoons pepper
2	(28-ounce) cans crushed red tomatoes
2	cups tomato juice
¼	cup brown sugar
1	can kidney beans, drained
1	can whole-kernel corn, drained
	Minced onion and plain yogurt for garnish

Heat 4 tablespoons oil in a large sauté pan over medium heat. Add the ground turkey and cook it all the way through, approximately 10 minutes. Salt and pepper the turkey lightly and put aside. Heat the remaining 2 tablespoons oil in a large pot over medium heat and sauté the onion and garlic until soft. Add the chili powder, cumin, oregano, red pepper flakes, salt, and pepper and stir. Add the tomatoes, juice, and brown sugar. Stir and bring to a boil and then turn down to a simmer. Simmer for about 10 minutes. Add the cooked turkey, kidney beans, and corn. Stir to combine and taste for seasoning. Garnish with the minced onions and plain yogurt.

MAKES 6 SERVINGS

Turkey Hash

A great way to use leftover turkey is by serving turkey hash topped with poached, fried, or scrambled eggs.

1	tablespoon vegetable oil
½	red bell pepper, seeded and diced
½	green bell pepper, seeded and diced
½	yellow bell pepper, seeded and diced
1	onion, diced
2	pounds cooked turkey, finely diced
1	sage sprig, chopped, or 1 teaspoon dried sage
1	tablespoon chopped fresh tarragon or 1 teaspoon dried tarragon
1	thyme sprig, chopped, or 1 teaspoon dried thyme
	Salt and pepper
2	cups leftover mashed potatoes
	Butter for cooking

Heat the oil in a medium-size sauté pan over medium heat. Sauté the red, green, and yellow peppers and the onions until they are soft, about 5 minutes. Add the turkey, sage, tarragon, thyme, and salt and pepper to taste. Cook for 1 to 2 minutes and pour the mixture into a mixing bowl. Stir in the potatoes. When cool, mix with your hands. Shape into patties. At this stage, you can wrap each patty individually in plastic wrap and freeze.

If you are going to use them immediately, heat about 2 teaspoons butter in a 4-inch sauté pan for individual patties. When the butter is hot, carefully spread the patty flat in the pan and turn down the heat a bit. Let one side brown—it will get crispy around the edges—and then flip it over and brown on the other side. For a larger batch of hash, heat up a cast iron skillet and add 4 tablespoons butter and 4 cups turkey hash. Pat the hash down in the pan, turn the heat down to medium, let the patty get crispy for about 8 minutes, and then flip over.

MAKES 10 TO 12 SMALL PATTIES

Award-Winning Venison Chili

As in the best beef chilies, Sissy's venison chili calls for the meat to be cut into tiny pieces rather than ground to a pulp. Its flavor stands out better that way, and small pieces give the chili a pleasing, rugged texture.

2	pounds venison		2	teaspoons ground black pepper
4	ounces bacon, diced		2	dried chipotle peppers, rehydrated and diced
2	tablespoons vegetable oil			
2	onions, diced		2	(28-ounce) cans crushed tomatoes
1	tablespoon minced garlic		¼	cup brown sugar
½	cup chili powder		1	(15-ounce) can black beans
1	tablespoon ground cumin			Chopped scallions or onions and sour cream for topping
2	teaspoons dried oregano			
1	teaspoon salt			

Smoke the venison on an outdoor grill over dampened wood chips for about 20 minutes. Smoke it just long enough for flavor, not to cook the meat. Remove the venison from the grill and set aside to chill. When cool dice it into very small pieces. Heat the diced bacon in a large sauté pan over medium heat. Render the fat from bacon. Leave the bacon and fat in the pan and add the venison. Stir the meat until it is thoroughly browned. Remove from the heat and set aside.

Heat the oil in a large pot over medium heat. Add the onion and garlic. Sauté until soft, about 5 minutes. Add the chili powder, cumin, oregano, salt, pepper, and chipotle peppers. Stir. Add the tomatoes and brown sugar. Bring up to a boil and, then turn down to a simmer. Simmer for about 10 minutes then add the venison and the black beans. Stir and taste for seasoning. Serve with toppings of chopped scallions or onions and sour cream.

MAKES 6 SERVINGS

Scallion Pancakes

A delicious side dish for brunch with scrambled eggs and sautéed spinach.

1	cup all-purpose flour
2½	teaspoons baking powder
½	teaspoon salt
2	eggs
1¼	cups milk
3	tablespoons butter, melted and cooled
½	cup scallions

Mix the flour, baking powder, and salt together. In another bowl, whisk together the eggs, milk, and butter. Slowly add the egg mixture to the flour mixture. Add the scallions. Drop dollops of the batter onto a hot griddle and cook as you would regular pancakes.

MAKES 4 TO 6 SERVINGS

Salmon Cakes

Cakes may seem like the thing to make when you have leftover cooked salmon—and they are a very good way to make the best of it—but if you want salmon cakes that are astoundingly moist and rich, buy the freshest fish you can find and poach it just before making the cakes. And don't skimp on the butter in your frying pan.

2	pounds poached salmon, flaked
2	baked potatoes, chilled and grated
1½	cups minced onion
2	celery ribs, minced
	Butter for sautéing
2	tablespoons mayonnaise
1	large egg
1	tablespoon Worcestershire sauce
1	teaspoon minced fresh dill
2	tablespoons capers, drained and minced
	Flour for dredging

Combine the salmon and potatoes lightly in a bowl. Sauté the onion and celery in a little butter. Cool and add to the salmon and potato. Add the mayonnaise, egg, Worcestershire sauce, dill, and capers. Mix together gently. Form into six patties. Dredge the patties in the flour and sauté them in hot butter.

MAKES 6 SERVINGS

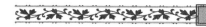 

Corned Beef Hash

Hash is a substantial dish suitable for breakfast, lunch, or dinner. It is a fundamental part of the cook's repertoire in New England, where nothing is wasted, including the corned beef left-over from last night's boiled dinner. You can use roast beef instead of corned beef if you like.

2	carrots
2	purple-top turnips
1	medium-large celery root
1	large Spanish onion
1	green bell pepper
2	plus 2 tablespoons vegetable oil
	Salt and pepper
9	small red potatoes
3	pounds cooked corned beef, shredded
	Butter for frying
	Poached eggs for serving (optional)

Preheat the oven to 350°F. Peel and coarsely chop the carrots, turnips, celery root, onion, and green pepper. Arrange them in a roasting pan and toss well with 2 tablespoons oil. Season to taste with the salt and pepper and roast them in the oven until they are soft, about 10 minutes. Roast the potatoes tossed with the remaining 2 tablespoons oil and the salt and pepper in a separate pan until cooked through, about 40 minutes. Combine the corned beef and vegetables (including the potatoes) in a food processor and pulse to blend. (You may have to do this in batches.) Transfer the mixture to a large mixing bowl, stir to blend well, and form into fairly large patties. (At this point the patties may be frozen and defrosted when needed.) When ready to cook, melt enough butter to cover the bottom of a large skillet and fry the patties over medium heat, browning on both sides. Top with a poached egg and serve.

MAKES 8 SERVINGS

Garlic Herb Corn Muffins

Savory muffins look great in the dinner-table bread basket and go especially well with a meal of ham, pork chops, or spiced beef.

1	cup all-purpose flour
1	cup cornmeal
1	to 1½ tablespoons sugar, or to taste
4	teaspoons baking soda
1½	teaspoons salt
¼	teaspoon chopped fresh thyme leaves
¼	teaspoon chopped fresh rosemary
¼	teaspoon chopped fresh marjoram
¼	teaspoon chopped fresh sage
2	eggs, lightly beaten
1	cup milk
4	tablespoons (½ stick) melted butter
4	roasted garlic cloves, puréed

Preheat the oven to 425°F. Sift the flour, cornmeal, sugar, baking soda, and salt together into a mixing bowl. Mix in the thyme, rosemary, marjoram, and sage. In a separate bowl whisk together the eggs, milk, butter, and garlic. Make a well in the center of the dry ingredients and pour in the egg mixture. Stir to a smooth batter. Fill a well-buttered muffin tin or corn-stick pan two-thirds full. Bake for 15 to 20 minutes or until nicely browned and baked through.

MAKES 6 MUFFINS

Mom's Corn Fritters

On the farm, we used to have 'corn day' late in the summer," Sissy recalls. "My dad would bring in bushels of fresh sweet corn, and all the ladies would come in and process it and bag it. At the end of the day, mom would make corn fritters. I so remember the taste. I can't make them quite like Mom's, but they're good!"

¼	cup all-purpose flour
½	teaspoon salt
1	teaspoon baking powder
1	tablespoon melted butter
½	cup buttermilk
3	eggs, beaten
2	cups fresh corn cut off the cob
4	cups canola oil
	Maple syrup

In a mixing bowl combine the flour, salt, baking powder, butter, buttermilk, and eggs. Stir in the corn. In a large skillet heat the oil over high heat until it reaches 300°F. Drop the batter into the oil by the tablespoonful and cook until the fritters are brown on one side. Turn carefully and brown the other side. Remove from the skillet and drain. Serve with maple syrup for breakfast or lunch.

MAKES 4 SERVINGS

Garlic Mozzarella Bread

Everybody's favorite and a staple of the Dorset Inn," is how Sissy describes her luxurious garlic mozzarella bread. With soup and salad, it is a full-service luncheon.

1	sub roll or demi-loaf, 6 to 8-inches long
2	(¼-inch-thick) slices mozzarella cheese, cut into quarters
½	cup Garlic Butter (recipe follows)

Preheat the oven to 350°F. Cut the bread into ½-slices, being careful not to cut all the way through the loaf. Put a piece of cheese in each slit. Spread the Garlic Butter over the top of the loaf. Bake on a baking sheet for 15 minutes, or until the cheese is melted and the bread is nicely browned on top.

MAKES ONE LOAF (8 SLICES)

Garlic Butter

10	garlic cloves
4	shallots
10	sprigs parsley, stemmed
2	teaspoons salt
2	teaspoons black pepper
2	cups (4 sticks) unsalted butter, softened

Mince the garlic, shallots, and parsley in a food processor. Transfer this mixture to a stand mixer and add the salt, pepper, and butter. Using the paddle attachment, whip until the butter is soft.

MAKES 2 CUPS

Sissy's Scones

How did this recipe come to be? "I had a lot of yogurt that I needed to use up," Sissy recalls. "So I thought, *let's see if I can make some scones.* When you have a lot of product on hand, you have to be inventive. To me, that is the creative part of cooking."

1½	cups all-purpose flour
1½	cups yellow cornmeal
⅓	cup plus 1 tablespoon sugar
½	teaspoon baking soda
¾	teaspoon salt
1½	sticks (¾ cup) unsalted butter, diced
4	teaspoons chopped dried fruit (cherries or apricots)
8	ounces maple yogurt (Old Chatham)
1	tablespoon melted butter

Preheat the oven to 400°F. Combine the flour, cornmeal, ⅓ cup sugar, baking soda, and salt in a large bowl. Add the diced butter and work the mixture with your fingers until it is the texture of crumbly cornmeal. Add the dried fruit and slowly work in the yogurt with your hands. The batter should be bread-dough consistency. Roll out the dough on a floured surface. Push it into a rectangular shape and cut into triangles. Place the scones on a greased baking sheet. Brush with the melted butter and sprinkle with the remaining 1 tablespoon sugar. Bake for about 10 minutes.

MAKES 12 SCONES

Bacon-Potato Pancakes

Potato pancakes are always a good thing. Potato pancakes that include bacon are even better. Any ordinary bacon will elevate this dish; but if you use high-quality, thick-sliced smokehouse bacon, it will soar.

3	Idaho baking potatoes
1	teaspoon salt
¼	pound bacon, diced
1	medium white onion, diced
	Black pepper (optional)
	Butter for sautéing

Cover the potatoes with water in a medium saucepan. Add the salt and bring to a boil over high heat. Reduce to a simmer and cook until just soft, approximately 20 minutes. Remove from the heat, drain, and let cool. While the potatoes are cooling, cook the diced bacon in a medium sauté pan over low heat until crisp. Drain the fat. When the potatoes are cool, peel and then grate them coarsely into a mixing bowl. Add the onion and bacon bits. Taste for seasoning, adding more salt and the pepper if desired. Form into patties as small or as large as you like. I usually make approximately 6-ounce patties. You can refrigerate them at this stage or cook them right away. Melt 1 tablespoon butter over high heat in a small sauté pan. When the pan is hot, add the potato pancake. Let brown on one side until crispy and then carefully turn over to brown on the other side. Continue the process until all the pancakes are cooked. Keep them warm on a tray in a warm oven.

MAKES 6 SERVINGS

Soups

Cream of Butternut Squash and Apple Soup

Cream of Chicken and Cucumber Soup

Cream of Mustard Soup

Lobster Bisque

Chilled Fresh Pea and Mint Soup

Purée of Carrot and Tomato Soup

Tomato Bisque

Carrot and White Bean Soup

Chilled Cucumber Soup

Mushroom Pumpkin Bisque

Red Potato Soup

Cream of Summer Squash and Basil Soup

Cream of Butternut Squash and Apple Soup

Yankee cooks make the most of the bell-shaped butternut squash, known for its dense, dark-orange flesh. While it is a winter vegetable, it stores well and is generally available year-round.

1	tablespoon vegetable oil
1	onion, sliced
1	medium butternut squash, peeled, seeded, and cut into chunks
2	McIntosh apples, peeled, cored, and diced
1	teaspoon salt
½	teaspoon allspice
½	teaspoon ground cinnamon
½	teaspoon cloves
1	cup cider
1	cup water or chicken stock
2	cups heavy cream
	Crème fraîche, minced apple, and minced parsley for garnish

Heat the oil in a medium-size pot over medium heat. When hot, add the onion and cook until just soft, about 5 minutes. Add the butternut squash and toss. Add the apple, salt, allspice, cinnamon, and cloves. Toss the mixture and then add the cider and water to cover. Bring to a boil, then reduce to a simmer, and cook until the squash is soft, about 20 minutes. Remove the squash mixture from the heat and purée it in a food processor. Return the puréed mixture to the pot and add the heavy cream. Heat on low until hot. Garnish with the crème fraîche, minced apple, and minced parsley.

MAKES 12 SERVINGS

Cream of Chicken and Cucumber Soup

You can easily adjust the nature of this creamy soup by using either all white meat or all dark or a combination of the two. All white meat is tea-room pleasant; all dark meat imparts a more sensuous savor.

2	tablespoons vegetable oil
1	small onion, sliced
4	cucumbers, peeled, seeded, and sliced
2	celery ribs, sliced
4	tablespoons chopped fresh dill
2	cups cooked chicken meat
4	cups chicken stock (see page 141)
	Salt and pepper

Béchamel Sauce

6	cups milk
6	tablespoons roux

Heat the oil in a medium-size pot over medium heat. Add the onion, cucumbers, and celery and sauté until just soft. Add the dill, chicken meat, stock, and salt and pepper to taste. Let simmer for 15 minutes.

In the meantime, make a béchamel. Scald the milk in a small saucepan. When hot, whisk in the roux. Keep stirring until the mixture thickens and starts to coat the spoon, about 15 to 20 minutes. Remove from the heat. Add the béchamel to the chicken mixture and keep stirring. Let simmer for a few minutes so the flavors can meld. Taste for seasoning.

MAKES 8 TO 10 SERVINGS

Cream of Mustard Soup

While chicken stock is the usual medium, vegetable stock makes this soup an excellent no-meat dish. The combination of smooth cream and sharp mustard creates a brilliant taste bud balancing act.

2	tablespoons vegetable oil
½	leek, white part only, sliced
1	onion, diced
1	carrot, peeled and diced
2	celery ribs, diced
1	cup Dijon mustard
2	sprigs fresh tarragon
2	sprigs fresh thyme
2	teaspoons salt
6	cups chicken stock (or mild vegetable stock)
6	tablespoons roux
1	pint heavy cream
	Bacon bits and scallions for garnish

Heat the oil in a medium-size pot over medium heat. Add the leek, onion, carrot, and celery, and sauté until transparent, approximately 5 minutes. Add the mustard, tarragon, thyme, salt, and chicken stock. Bring to a boil and then reduce to a simmer for about 30 minutes until the vegetables are soft. Strain into another pot and place over medium-low heat. Whisk in the roux. Simmer and stir until the mixture thickens. Add the heavy cream and simmer until the flavors are well blended. Serve garnished with bacon bits and a thin julienne of scallions.

MAKES 8 TO 10 SERVINGS

SLOW FOOD

Slow food is the opposite of fast food. It is regional, seasonal, and fresh. Its groceries come from small farms and locally-owned stores. A slow-food meal takes a while to cook, and most people take their sweet time eating it.

In a sense, there has always been slow food, and "progress" has always been about speeding it up. In fact, the Slow Food Movement was ignited in response to the fast food industry. In 1986 McDonald's announced plans to build one of its restaurants at the base of the Spanish Steps in Rome. Italian author Carlo Petrini led a campaign against the golden arches and industrialized homogeneity they symbolize. Petrini and his comrades formed the "International Movement for the Defense and the Right to Pleasure" and issued a manifesto in praise of the sensual pleasure and prolonged enjoyment of elaborate meals, fine wine, and rambling conversation. Its members meet to learn about food and culinary culture, to share relaxed meals and tastings, and to do what they can to promote appreciation of local produce and pleasurable dining.

You won't find a restaurant that exemplifies these principles more delightfully than the Dorset Inn. "I feel very much a part of the Slow Food Movement," Sissy Hicks told us in the kitchen one day as she prepared shanks from charro lambs raised locally (but with bloodlines tracing back to ancient Navajo flocks in the Southwest). "So much of what the movement stands for has been what I have believed in all along: comfort food, home cooking, natural simplicity.

"Here at the inn, I try to be as local and seasonal as possible. We stay away from imported produce and use what is harvested in New England: peas, beans, and corn in the summer. When the corn comes in like crazy and is at its most flavorful, I freeze it so we can have that good taste through the winter and serve corn fritters with maple syrup. Artisan cheeses are always available, and of course we have wonderful North Atlantic seafood."

Some people are shocked when they first taste the organic beef Sissy buys from a Vermont farm. "It has a totally different flavor than the bland meat most people know," she says. "I age it a couple of weeks, and it has a gamy quality, but it is the real thing. Once you've had it, you know there is nothing better."

Sissy told us that she has a list of regular customers she calls when certain seasonal specialties become available: shad roe in late April, soft shell crabs in May, and strawberries (for classic shortcake) in June. One of the most exciting times is the evanescent fiddlehead fern season. Sissy told us that fiddleheads appear in the spring and are ready to pick for no more than a day or two. There is a great spot for fiddleheads, just off Route 7. There are thousands of them!

"When the time is right, we go on fiddlehead alert," Sissy said, explaining that she sautés them in lemon butter and serves them with pasta, in soups, and in breakfast omelets.

Sissy confided that sometimes she fantasizes about running a restaurant with a mere twenty seats. "I could do everything myself," she beamed. Every meal would be made of food that she would grow or find, and each plate would be hand-tailored to the person who would eat it. In so many ways that fantasy comes true at the Dorset Inn. "I don't see this as a restaurant," she summarized. "I am the country inn experience. You have breakfast, you go out for a stroll and enjoy Vermont. You return for lunch or tea and have a nap or read on the front porch. Breathe the good air. And at twilight, you come in and enjoy a relaxing dinner. That's my message: slow down, relax, eat in peace."

Nellie the Pig, shown here at a Slow Food dinner, helps round up stray apples in the orchards of cidermakers Rich and Kristin Ford of Sauvie Island, Oregon. Photo courtesy of Katherine Deumling.

Lobster Bisque

The nomenclature of Downeast soup is complex and confusing. There are chowders, stews, soups, and bisques, and subcategories within each of those. Of all of them, bisque is the richest. Cream plus sherry plus lobster equals one of the most extravagant-tasting dishes imaginable.

6	cooked lobster carcasses (see note)
6	tablespoons butter
1	large carrot, peeled and diced
2	celery ribs, diced
1	onion, peeled and sliced
1	leek, sliced
½	cup tomato paste
4	tablespoons roux
2	tablespoons chopped fresh tarragon
2	cups dry sherry
2	quarts (8 cups) heavy cream
	Pinch of cayenne
	Salt and pepper

Remove and discard the hard shell from the lobster bodies. Melt the butter in a large pot, and sauté the carrot, celery, onion, and leek until the vegetables are soft. Add the lobster carcasses and pound them with a mallet until they break down. Add the tomato paste, roux, tarragon, and sherry. Stir everything together and simmer for about 10 minutes, or until the mixture has reduced by half. Add the heavy cream and continue simmering until this reduces a bit. Add the cayenne and salt and pepper to taste. Look for a slightly thickened consistency that will coat the back of the spoon. Using a ladle, pour the soup through a strainer and crush the lobster carcasses to extract as much juice as possible.

MAKES 10 TO 12 SERVINGS

Note: Remove the lobster meat from the claws and tail and use it for a bouillabaise or lobster salad. Use the remaining body for this bisque.

Chilled Fresh Pea and Mint Soup

Cool and refreshing and yet substantial (especially if heavy cream is used), fresh pea and mint soup is a summer favorite.

2	tablespoons vegetable oil
1	medium onion, diced
2	medium Idaho potatoes, peeled and diced
2	teaspoons salt
1	teaspoon black pepper
8	cups chicken stock
4	cups fresh or frozen peas
1 ½	cups mint leaves, peppermint, or spearmint, plus some for garnish
1	cup heavy cream (optional)
	Crème fraîche for garnish

Heat the oil over low heat in a medium saucepan. Add the diced onion, stir, and cook about 5 minutes or until the onions are soft. Add the potatoes and the salt and pepper. Add the chicken stock and bring to a boil; then reduce the heat to a simmer for about 10 minutes until the potatoes are just beginning to soften. Drop in the peas and mint, stir, and quickly bring the soup back to a boil for about 3 minutes. Purée the soup right away and chill until ready to serve. When ready to serve, you can add heavy cream if you wish. Garnish with a dollop of crème fraîche and minced mint.

MAKES 8 TO 10 SERVINGS

Purée of Carrot and Tomato Soup

Tomato soup is good, but the salubrious addition of carrots creates a dish of simple satisfaction welcome at lunch (or supper) year-round.

2	tablespoons vegetable oil
1	medium onion, peeled and sliced
3	carrots, peeled and sliced
2	tablespoons minced fresh dill
1	(28-ounce) can whole tomatoes in juice
	Salt and pepper

Heat the oil in a medium-size, stainless steel pot. Add the onion and cook until soft, about 5 minutes. Add the carrots and dill and toss with the onion. Add the tomatoes and juice. Fill the tomato can with cold water and add the water to the pot. Bring to a boil and reduce to a simmer for about 30 minutes or until the carrots are soft. Remove from the heat and purée the soup in a food processor or blender. Season to taste with the salt and pepper.

MAKES 4 TO 6 SERVINGS

Tomato Bisque

We always like being reminded that tomatoes are a fruit, at least botanically (their flesh covers seeds); and their flavor can have a certain sweetness that is here brought out by the addition of sugar.

2	pounds tomatoes, quartered
2	celery ribs, sliced
1	onion, chopped
2	whole cloves
2	cups water
4	tablespoons roux
2	tablespoons sugar
	Fresh basil for garnish

Combine the tomatoes, celery, onion, cloves, and water in a stainless steel pot, cover, and bring to a boil over medium heat; reduce to a simmer. Simmer for about 30 minutes and remove from the heat. Put the soup through a food mill or strainer and return the soup to the pot. Whisk in the roux and add the sugar. (The sugar reacts with the acid and gives just a touch of sweetness.) Garnish with the fresh basil.

MAKES 6 TO 8 SERVINGS

Carrot and White Bean Soup

Sissy calls this, "A great vegetarian soup with an infusion of fresh rosemary and thyme. It is so hearty it could be a main course with a good baguette and a salad."

1	medium onion, minced
1	teaspoon minced garlic
1	tablespoon butter
2	sprigs thyme
1	sprig rosemary
2	cups diced carrots
2	cups great Northern beans, soaked overnight
9	cups water
	Salt and pepper

In a 4-quart stockpot over medium heat cook the onion and garlic in the butter until soft. Add the thyme, rosemary, carrots, beans, water, and salt and pepper to taste. Bring to a boil, reduce the heat, and simmer for about 2 hours or until the beans are soft. Remove the sprigs of thyme and rosemary. (All the leaves will have fallen off.) Cool the soup slightly and purée in a food processor.

MAKES 8 TO 12 SERVINGS

Chilled Cucumber Soup

A very refreshing soup on a hot summer evening.

8	*cucumbers, peeled and seeded*
1	*quart (4 cups) plain yogurt*
2	*cups buttermilk*
¼	*cup minced dill*
	Juice of 2 lemons
10	*dashes Tabasco*
	Salt and pepper

   In a food processor purée 4 cucumbers and place them in a mixing bowl. Grate the remaining 4 cucumbers, wrap with cheesecloth or paper towels, and squeeze out the liquid. Add them to the bowl. Whisk or stir in the yogurt, buttermilk, dill, lemon juice, and Tabasco. Add the salt and pepper to taste. Chill to serve.

MAKES 6 SERVINGS

Mushroom Pumpkin Bisque

When we were discussing this recipe with Sissy, she reminded us that the part of Pennsylvania where she grew up is the mushroom capital of the world. She said that this bisque was inspired by one that she and her mother enjoyed back home. "In the fall, when pumpkins are in season, it is really special," she notes.

2	tablespoons butter
3	shallots, sliced
4	cups sliced cremini mushrooms
2	teaspoons fresh thyme leaves
½	teaspoon cumin
¼	teaspoon cardamom
	Salt and pepper
½	cup dry sherry
4½	cups chicken stock
3	cups pumpkin purée
1	cup heavy cream

Melt the butter in a medium-size saucepan and sauté the shallots, mushrooms, and thyme for about 5 minutes over medium heat. Add the cumin, cardamom, salt and pepper to taste, and sherry; reduce for about 5 minutes. Add the chicken stock and pumpkin purée and simmer for about 10 minutes. Add the heavy cream and simmer until warm.

MAKES 6 SERVINGS

 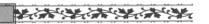

Red Potato Soup

Sissy recommends using Red Bliss potatoes for this soup, especially mid-summer when they are at their most flavorful. She gets hers from Hebela Farms in Rutland and a fellow there she calls the Spud Man.

2	tablespoons butter
1	medium onion, chopped
1	small leek with some of the green, chopped
2	pounds red potatoes, unpeeled and quartered
2½	cups chicken stock
2	cups half-and-half
2	cups heavy cream
	Salt and pepper

In a 4-quart stockpot melt the butter over low heat and sauté the onion and leek until soft. Add the potatoes and chicken stock and bring to a boil. Reduce the heat and simmer until the potatoes are soft. Add the half-and-half, heavy cream, and salt and pepper to taste. Bring back to a simmer. Remove from the heat and cool slightly. Purée in a food processor or blender. Serve hot or cold.

MAKES 6 SERVINGS

Cream of Summer Squash and Basil Soup

It is common for Sissy's friends from Someday Farm—a local organic farm—to stop by the back door of the Dorset Inn's kitchen and drop off fruits, vegetables, and herbs that they've grown. In the summer there is a surplus of squash—put to good use with fresh basil in this creamy soup.

1	cup chopped onion
2	tablespoons olive oil
6	cups sliced summer squash
¼	cup minced basil plus 6 leaves for garnish
2	teaspoons salt
1	teaspoon pepper
4	cups water or chicken stock
½	cup white wine
1	quart (4 cups) heavy cream
	Crème fraîche

In a large stockpot sauté the onion in olive oil over medium heat until wilted. Add the summer squash, ¼ cup minced basil, salt, and pepper and sauté until translucent. Add the stock and the wine, bring just to a boil, and let simmer for 10 minutes. Add the heavy cream and simmer for another 10 minutes. Take the pot off the heat and purée the soup in a food processor. Taste for seasoning. Garnish with the crème fraîche and the remaining 6 basil leaves.

MAKES 6 SERVINGS

Salads & Dressings

Coleslaw

Warm Chicken Tenderloin Salad

Arugula and Portobello Mushroom Salad

Roasted Red Beet Salad

Autumn Cobb Salad

Spinach Salad with Orange Curry, Flax Oil Dressing

Butternut Squash, Apple, and Fennel Salad

Country Dressing

Basil Vinaigrette

Stilton Dressing

Sun-Dried Tomato Vinaigrette

Caesar Dressing

Raspberry Vinaigrette

Coleslaw

Creamy, sweet-tangy slaw is not something you want to make fresh and serve right away. A few hours or overnight in the refrigerator allows its wide-ranging flavors to reach perfect harmony.

1	medium head white cabbage, shaved paper thin with a very sharp knife
1	medium onion, diced
1	carrot, coarsely grated
1	green pepper, diced
	Salt and pepper

Dressing

1	cup mayonnaise
¼	cup cider vinegar
¼	cup sugar
	Celery salt (optional)

Place the cabbage, onion, carrot, and green pepper in a large mixing bowl and lightly salt and pepper to taste.

To make the dressing, whisk together the mayonnaise, vinegar, sugar, and celery salt, if using, in a small bowl. Pour the dressing over the cabbage and toss. Refrigerate until ready to use. This will hold for several days—the longer it sits, the more flavorful it becomes.

MAKES 6 TO 8 SERVINGS

Warm Chicken Tenderloin Salad

The concept of warm fried chicken on a cool salad is one that makes us happy for culinary progress. A dish that didn't exist a few decades ago, it is now a favorite lunch item from California to the Atlantic Ocean. We love Sissy's inclusion of mushrooms and walnuts, both of which add not only flavor but textural variety.

30	chicken tenders
2	cups all-purpose flour
	Salt and pepper
12	plus 4 tablespoons vegetable or olive oil
12	button or shiitake mushrooms, sliced
1	pound mixed lettuce
3	tomatoes, cut into 18 wedges
	Sprinkle of chopped walnuts
	Balsamic vinaigrette

Dredge the chicken tenders in the flour seasoned with the salt and pepper to taste. Heat 4 tablespoons oil in a medium-size sauté pan over high heat. Working in batches, arrange the tenders in a single layer to brown on one side. Turn over and brown the other side. Lower the heat. Sauté the tenders until cooked through, about 5 minutes. Put the cooked tenders in a small tray to stay warm in the oven on very low heat while cooking the remaining tenders. Wipe out the sauté pan between batches. When you have finished with the tenders, sauté the mushrooms. Toss and lightly coat the lettuce with some Balsamic Vinaigrette in a large mixing bowl. Divide the lettuce among six plates, adding the tomato wedges as garnish. In the same mixing bowl, toss the tenders and the mushrooms in some additional Balsamic Dressing. Arrange the tenders and mushrooms on top of the lettuce. Sprinkle with the walnuts.

MAKES 6 SERVINGS

Arugula and Portobello Mushroom Salad

This is a favorite of Sissy's. She likes "the arugula's spicy pepperiness combined with the earthy flavor of the grilled portobellos and the subtle flavor of the Asiago." She notes that Asiago is very similar to Parmesan when paired with mushrooms.

---

3   *portobello mushrooms, stems removed*
       Olive oil for brushing mushrooms
2   *bunches arugula, washed thoroughly*

Roasted Garlic Vinaigrette

2   *garlic cloves, peeled and roasted*
4   *tablespoons balsamic vinegar*
1   *teaspoon salt*
1   *cup olive oil*

4   *ounces Asiago cheese, shaved with a potato peeler*

Brush the mushrooms with the oil and grill them, or place in a 350°F oven until just soft, about 8 minutes. Slice ½ inch thick.

Prepare the Roasted Garlic Vinaigrette. Combine the garlic, vinegar, and salt in a food processor. While processing, slowly add the oil in a steady stream until well mixed.

Toss the arugula in the viniagrette. Arrange the arugula on plates with the sliced mushrooms and top with the shaved cheese. The garlic vinaigrette melds the flavors in this salad.

MAKE 4 TO 6 SERVINGS

Note: If you want to serve this as a main luncheon dish, some quinoa (a couscous-like grain found in natural food stores) tossed in the salad makes it very substantial.

Roasted Red Beet Salad

Made with local goat cheese from Bardwell Farm, this is a dark-hued salad for when beets are in season in the fall and winter. It is a great combination of the earthy taste of beets and pungent goat cheese.

3	pounds medium red beets or a combo of red and yellow
1	teaspoon chopped fresh rosemary
1	teaspoon chopped fresh sage
1	teaspoon chopped fresh thyme
1	teaspoon chopped fresh tarragon
2	shallots, chopped
¼	cup vegetable oil

Herbed Goat Cheese Balls

6	ounces plain goat cheese
¼	cup heavy cream
1	tablespoon mixed chopped fresh sage, rosemary, thyme, and tarragon
1	tablespoon lemon juice.

Pistachio Vinaigrette

1	cup pistachios, toasted and minced
¼	cup rice wine vinegar
¼	cup cider vinegar
2	tablespoons orange juice
2	teaspoons salt
1	teaspoon pepper
1 ½	cups olive oil

½	pound mixed greens

66

Preheat the oven to 350°F. Toss the whole beets in the rosemary, sage, thyme, tarragon, shallots, and oil. Place in a roasting pan and cover with foil. Roast for 1½ hours or until soft to the touch. Let cool, covered, for about 15 minutes. (The beets will peel easily.)

While the beets are roasting make the Herbed Goat Cheese Balls. Mix the goat cheese, heavy cream, fresh herb mix, and lemon juice in a small mixing bowl with a wooden spoon. With your hands roll into small balls, place on a platter, and chill until ready to use.

For the Pistachio Vinaigrette, in a medium-size mixing bowl, combine the pistachios, vinegars, orange juice, salt, and pepper. Slowly whisk in the oil until well blended.

To arrange the salad, peel and slice the beets into ¼ inch slices. Make a ring of six beet slices around each plate. Place the greens in the middle with a couple of the Herbed Goat Cheese Balls on top. Drizzle some of the Pistachio Vinaigrette over all.

MAKES 6 SERVINGS

Autumn Cobb Salad

Here is a seasonal alternative to the Cobb salad I serve in the spring and summer," Sissy says. The combination of squash, celery root and maple vinaigrette gives it a well-blended autumn flavor. She uses Boucher Farm's version of Gorgonzola, which they call Gore-Dawn-zola after proprietor Dawn Morin-Boucher.

3	cups butternut squash, diced and roasted with maple syrup, salt, and pepper.
3	cups julienned raw zucchini
3	cups julienned celery root
1	Granny Smith apple, thinly sliced
1	small red onion, peeled and julienned
1	cup crumbled Gorgonzola cheese

Maple Vinaigrette

1	shallot, minced
1	cup maple syrup
½	cup apple cider vinegar
2½	cups vegetable oil
	Mixed greens for 6 large salads

In a large mixing bowl toss together the squash, zucchini, celery root, apple, onion, and Gorgonzola cheese.

Prepare the Maple Vinaigrette. In a mixing bowl combine the shallot, syrup, and vinegar. Slowly add the oil while whisking vigorously. Mix in ½ cup of the Maple Vinaigrette and serve over the mixed greens.

MAKES 6 SERVINGS

Spinach Salad with Orange Curry, Flax Oil Dressing

Flax oil is the basis of this light, healthy dressing. It is based on Sissy's desire to come up with an alternative to the typical bacon dressing served on spinach salads. It is a dish for vegetarians.

Dressing

1	shallot, diced
1	teaspoon curry powder
2	tablespoons fresh orange juice
2	tablespoons cider vinegar
1	teaspoon salt
½	teaspoon black pepper
1	cup flax oil

Salad

1	pound spinach, stemmed and washed
½	red onion, sliced
1	orange, peeled and sectioned
1	cup crumbled Stilton cheese (or Boucher Farm Blue Cheese)
½	cup finely chopped sunflower seeds

For the dressing, mix together in a small bowl the shallot, curry powder, orange juice, vinegar, salt, and pepper. Slowly whisk in the flax oil.

For the salad, in a large bowl toss together the spinach, onion, orange, cheese, and sunflower seeds and mix with ¼ cup of the dressing.

MAKES 6 SERVINGS

SUMMER IN VERMONT

Dorset's reputation as a relaxing and scenic seasonal residence traces to a particular couple, time, and place," Tyler Resch observed in his definitive history *Dorset*. The couple was George and Elizabeth Prentiss, New Yorkers who first came to town in 1866. They started their affair with Dorset in rented rooms; in 1868, after falling in love with the woods and mountains, they built a cottage of their own.

For ten years, until Mrs. Prentiss's death, the couple summered in Dorset. "Once out of the city, she was like a bird let loose from its cage," Mr. Prentiss wrote about his wife. In their wake came generations of "summer people" for whom two or three months of hiking, bicycling, picnicking, horseback riding, automobiling, or just plain relaxing in the picture-pretty Vermont town became a welcome respite from city life. Many came to town on their physicians' recommendation. Located in the highest valley between New York and Montreal, Dorset was famous for its crisp mountain air. And no doubt, the town's sidewalks, made of regal marble from local quarries, had their own allure for class-conscious city folk.

By 1900 Dorset had nine boarding houses and two hotels, including the Barrows House and the Dorset Inn (then known as the Washington Hotel). It cost two dollars per day to stay in one of the hotels, and another dollar for board. Increasingly, people who could afford to do so bought or built homes in Dorset. By World War II, one-fifth of the town's citizens were summer people with primary residence somewhere else.

Their presence was not necessarily welcomed by Dorset natives. In 1943 *Harper's Magazine* editor John Kouwenhoven delivered a talk at the Dorset Field Club titled "Whose Town Is It?" Kouwenhoven, himself a relative newcomer who had arrived in Dorset six years earlier, described a social rift between full-time residents and those he referred to as infiltrators. He maintained that townsfolk resented wealthy summer interlopers who seemed to have nothing but leisure time. He noted that twelve of the eighteen houses around the village green were empty all winter. In his town history, Tyler Resch quotes a 1972 article by longtime Dorset native William Gilbert lamenting "the suburbanization of Dorset" by well-to-do people from elsewhere. Development of Stratton, Bromley, and Magic Mountain ski lifts in the 1950s attracted even more out-of-towners to the area, year-round.

No one promoted Dorset as a leisure-time destination more enthusiastically than Richard Marston Campbell, himself a native whose family came to town in 1886 when he was five years old. After writing three editions of a pamphlet titled "Dorset, Vermont, as a Summer Home," Campbell wrote "Dorset Among the Mountains Green, Vermont in 1924." In it he rhapsodized about the assets of the village:

> First, the Pure Mountain Air and the Wonderful Scenery; second, the freedom of the social life and its informal simplicity; Artists, Authors, Divines, Bankers, Physicians, Lawyers, Manufacturers, Merchants, and Educators are all represented and all unite in singing the praises of Dorset and its wonderful attractions. Like Niagara Falls, it grows on one as one takes in its Natural Beauties.

Butternut Squash, Apple, and Fennel Salad

Sissy describes this salad as "a real seasonal dish—a blend of fall flavors."

3	cups diced butternut squash, roasted with maple syrup, salt, and pepper
½	fennel bulb, julienned (save some of the fronds to toss in)
1	Granny Smith apple, thinly sliced, unpeeled
½	red onion, julienned
½	cup Maple Vinaigrette

Maple Vinaigrette

1	minced shallot
½	cup apple cider vinegar
1	cup maple syrup (Grade B)
1	teaspoon salt
½	teaspoon black pepper
2½	cups vegetable oil
½	pound mixed greens

In a large salad bowl toss together the squash, fennel, apple, and onion.

For the maple vinaigrette, in a medium-size mixing bowl combine the shallot, vinegar, syrup, salt, and pepper. Slowly whisk in the vegetable oil until well blended. Pour the dressing over the squash mixture and toss. Serve over the mixed greens.

MAKES 6 SERVINGS

Country Dressing

This is a zesty, creamy dressing that is wonderful for salads. Everyone loves this dressing, especially Nuni, for its combination of flavors.

½	leek, diced
½	carrot, peeled and diced
1	parsley sprig, stemmed
2	egg yolks
1	tablespoon Dijon mustard
¼	cup raspberry vinegar
¼	cup white vinegar
1	teaspoon salt
2	tablespoons honey
½	teaspoon pepper
1½	cups vegetable oil

Combine the leek, carrot, parsley, egg yolks, mustard, vinegars, salt, honey, and pepper in a food processor. With the machine turned on, slowly add the oil and process until blended.

MAKES ABOUT 3 CUPS

Basil Vinaigrette

Here is a vinaigrette to make when basil can be clipped fresh in the summer. We would suggest experimenting with different basils: lemon basil, Thai basil, West Indian basil. This is a great dressing for a summer tomato and mozzarella cheese salad.

¼	cup white vinegar
½	cup Dijon mustard
4	garlic cloves
½	cup fresh basil
2	cups olive oil

Combine the vinegar, mustard, garlic, and basil in a food processor. With the machine running, slowly add the oil and process until well blended.

MAKES ABOUT 3 CUPS

Stilton Dressing

A delicious way to tease the tongue: creamy mayonnaise and sour cream mixed with sharp Stilton cheese. The recipe also works well with Boucher Farms blue cheese.

2	cups mayonnaise
1	cup sour cream
¼	cup white vinegar
	Salt and white pepper
1	cup Stilton cheese, crumbled (or Boucher Farms Blue Cheese)

In a large bowl combine the mayonnaise, sour cream, vinegar, and salt and pepper to taste. Stir in the Stilton, one handful at a time. Blend well.

MAKES 4 CUPS

Sun-Dried Tomato Vinaigrette

A salad dressing with heavy consistency, this is great with a summer salad of grilled egg-plant, zucchini, peppers, and mozzarella cheese or with lettuce, Asiago cheese, prosciutto, and red onion.

1	cup sun-dried tomatoes, rehydrated
2	shallots
3	garlic cloves
9	basil leaves
1	tablespoon balsamic vinegar
2	cups olive oil
	Salt and pepper

Combine the sun-dried tomatoes, shallots, garlic, basil, and vinegar in a food processor. With the machine running, slowly add the oil. Add the salt and pepper to taste.

MAKES ABOUT 3 CUPS

Caesar Dressing

The traditional method of preparing Caesar dressing is in the bowl where the salad will be mixed. Here's a much more convenient way to do it ahead of time and have it ready for the salad when it's time to toss.

6	garlic cloves
2	ounces anchovies
1	tablespoon Dijon mustard
½	tablespoon Worcestershire sauce
½	tablespoon dry mustard
3	egg yolks
1½	cups vegetable oil
¼	cup water
½	cup grated Parmesan cheese
	Juice of 1 lemon
	Salt and pepper

In a food processor blend the garlic cloves, anchovies, Dijon mustard, Worcestershire sauce, dry mustard, and egg yolks into a paste. While the machine is running, slowly add the oil. Then add the water and quickly pulse in the Parmesan cheese and lemon juice. Season to taste with the salt and pepper.

MAKES ABOUT 4 CUPS

Raspberry Vinaigrette

¼	cup raspberry vinegar
⅛	cup dry sherry (Dry Sak, for example)
4	sprigs parsley
1	shallot
1	teaspoon dry mustard
1½	cups olive oil
	Salt and pepper

Combine the vinegar, sherry, parsley, shallot, and mustard in a food processor. With the machine running, slowly add the oil. Add the salt and pepper to taste.

MAKES ABOUT 2 CUPS

Poultry

Duck Confit

Duck Risotto

Sautéed Chicken Livers

Stuffed Breasts of Chicken

Turkey Croquettes

Pine Nut Crusted Chicken Breast

Turkey Burger

Duck Confit

At the Dorset Inn, duck confit is served with plum chutney (see page 137), wild rice, and braised red cabbage. Sissy explains that "Confit, a specialty of Gascony, is an ancient method of preserving meat and poultry—salted and slowly cooked in its own fat, which acts as a sealant and preservative."

3	*ducks, 3½ to 4½ pounds each, boned and quartered (reserve the bones for duck stock)*
	Salt and pepper
6	*garlic cloves*
1	*sprig sage, chopped, or 1 teaspoon dried sage*
1	*sprig tarragon, chopped, or 1 teaspoon dried tarragon*
1	*sprig rosemary, chopped, or 1 teaspoon dried rosemary*
1	*sprig thyme, chopped, or 1 teaspoon dried thyme*
	Canola oil, enough to cover

Preheat the oven to 300°F. Season the ducks with the salt and pepper to taste and place them in an ovenproof casserole dish. Add the garlic, sage, tarragon, rosemary, and thyme and enough oil to cover. Bake for 3 hours or until slightly brown and the duck is tender.

MAKES 8 TO 10 SERVINGS

Note: If not using right away, store this, covered in a refrigerator, for up to two weeks. Be sure to store the fat with the duck. When ready to use, remove the duck from the fat, scraping off the excess. Bake at 400°F for 15 to 20 minutes or until the meat is heated through and the skin is crispy.

Duck Risotto

What a special-occasion treat! It takes some effort to roast the duck, then more to make the risotto, but the result is a company's coming meal. Sissy makes this using leftover Duck Confit on page 81.

Risotto		Duck	
1	large white onion, diced	2	tablespoons vegetable oil
3	garlic cloves, minced	2	shallots, sliced
2	tablespoons melted butter	1	cup sliced shiitake mushrooms
1	pound or 2 cups Arborio rice	1	cup sliced oyster mushrooms
1	teaspoon salt	1	tablespoon minced fresh rosemary
¼	teaspoon pepper	1	tablespoon minced fresh sage
¼	cup white wine	2	poblano peppers, roasted, peeled and julienned
3	to 4 cups duck or chicken stock (see pages 144 or 141)	1	roasted duck, meat pulled from the bones or leftover Duck Confit
		1	cup duck stock (see page 144)
		¼	cup grated Asiago cheese

For the risotto, sauté the onions and garlic in the butter over very low heat until wilted. Add the rice, salt, and pepper and stir until thoroughly coated. Add the white wine and reduce by half. Add the chicken stock ½ cup at a time, stirring the mixture continuously. All the liquid should be absorbed before adding more stock. This labor-intensive technique results in a rice that is delectably creamy while the grains remain separate and firm.

For the duck, heat the oil in a medium saucepan over medium heat. Add the shallots, mushrooms, rosemary, sage, and peppers. Sauté until the mushrooms and shallots are soft. Add the duck and toss with the risotto and duck stock. Add the cheese. This should be a fairly loose mixture.

MAKES 6 SERVINGS

Sautéed Chicken Livers

Fresh, fresh livers, sautéed until crisp, are really delectable," Sissy says. "Like calf livers, chicken liver has passionate devotees." Sissy serves sautéed chicken livers on puff pastry because she believes the pastry's crispness complements the richness of the liver. In lieu of puff pastry, toasted French bread will fill the bill.

1	(17.3–ounce) box Pepperidge Farm puff pastry
2	pounds fresh chicken livers, about five per person
1	cup flour for dredging
	Salt and pepper
4	tablespoons (½ stick) butter
	Madeira Sauce (see page 132)

Prepare the puff pastry according to package directions.

Dredge the chicken livers in the flour and season with the salt and pepper to taste. Sauté the livers in hot butter for 4 to 6 minutes, until brown, but still pink inside. Just before the livers are done, deglaze with some Madeira Sauce then spoon them over the puff pastry. Serve with Madeira Sauce over and under the sautéed chicken livers.

MAKES 8 SERVINGS

Stuffed Breasts of Chicken

Creamy Brie stuffing makes chicken a luxury item. Sissy suggests serving it with brown basmati rice. She also notes that the pear and cider sauce can be made well ahead of time, even the day before, and refrigerated until the meal is prepared. At the Dorset Inn, this recipe is made with Misty Knoll organic chickens. It is especially welcome in the fall when cider and pears are in season.

Pear and Cider Sauce

2	tablespoons (¼ stick) butter
2	shallots
3	ripe Bosc pears, peeled, seeded, and cut into chunks
4	sage leaves
¼	cup applejack or apple brandy
4	cups cider

Creamy Brie Stuffing

6	ounces Brie cheese, rind removed
¼	teaspoon coriander
1	shallot, minced
1	teaspoon minced parsley
3	boneless chicken breasts, cut in half
½	cup all-purpose flour
	Salt and pepper
2	tablespoons vegetable oil

For the Pear and Cider Sauce, melt the butter in a medium-size saucepan over medium heat. Add the shallots and cook for 3 minutes or until soft. Add the pears and sage leaves and toss them quickly and briefly. Add the brandy. Ignite it and let the alcohol burn off. This will flame up, so be very careful. (I have singed my eyelashes.) Once the applejack has reduced a bit, add the cider. Bring to a boil and turn down the heat to a simmer. Simmer uncovered for about 30 minutes. This should reduce a bit. The pears will be soft. Purée them in a food processor. Put any remaining sauce in a container and store in the refrigerator for up to four weeks. The sage gives the sauce a little earthy flavor.

While the sauce simmers, prepare the creamy brie stuffing. Mix the Brie, coriander, shallot, and parsley together in a small bowl. To prepare the chicken breasts for stuffing, using a sharp knife or a boning knife (or have your butcher do it for you), make a slice in the thicker side to form a pocket. Divide the cheese mixture evenly among the chicken breasts. This can be made a day ahead and the chicken refrigerated until ready for use.

When ready to cook, preheat the oven to 350°F. Dredge the breasts in the flour seasoned with the salt and pepper to taste and shake off the excess. Heat the oil in a large sauté pan on medium heat. Brown the breasts on both sides for approximately 4 minutes per side and transfer them to a small roasting pan. Bake in the oven for about 10 minutes. Serve the chicken with the pear sauce.

MAKES 6 SERVINGS

Turkey Croquettes

Sissy says that Thanksgiving is her favorite meal, mostly because of all the accompanying vegetables and potatoes. She especially likes turkey croquettes because they are "like the turkey meal all in one." They are so popular that they are always on the menu.

2	cups cooked turkey, even all those tiny scraps, diced
1	cup stuffing
¼	cup vegetable oil
1	onion, sliced
1	celery rib, chopped
½	leek, sliced
½	teaspoon dried sage
½	teaspoon dried thyme
½	teaspoon tarragon
1	cup turkey gravy, or, if there isn't any left over, use chicken stock with 2 tablespoons roux
1	cup all-purpose flour
4	eggs, beaten with a little water
2	cups breadcrumbs
	Canola oil for frying

Cranberry Sauce

1	pound sugar
2	cups water
1	pound cranberries
1	orange, chopped

Put the turkey meat and the stuffing in a large mixing bowl. Heat the vegetable oil in a medium-size saucepan over medium heat and sauté the onion, celery, leek, sage, thyme, and tarragon until just soft, approximately 5 minutes. Let cool to room temperature, and then add to the turkey and stuffing mixture. Toss with your hands. Put the entire mixture in a food processor and pulse to chop coarsely; do not purée. The croquettes are best with some texture. Put the mixture back into the mixing bowl and add the gravy. This will bind the mixture, so you will now be able to form little golf-ball-size croquettes.

In a cast-iron skillet or heavy saucepan, pour enough canola oil to measure two inches and heat over medium-high heat (350°F).

Put the flour, eggs, and breadcrumbs into three separate bowls. Roll each croquette in the flour, shaking off the excess. Then dip each croquette in the egg mixture, and then roll in the breadcrumbs until evenly coated. Drop the croquettes, one at a time, into the oil. (Be careful because the oil will bubble and splatter.) Cook the croquettes until brown, about 5 minutes.

Prepare the Cranberry Sauce. Bring the sugar and water to a boil in a saucepan over medium-high heat. Add the cranberries and orange. Simmer until the cranberries just begin to split open. Cool to room temperature, then refrigerate. Serve the croquettes with the Cranberry Sauce on the side.

MAKES 6 TO 8 SERVINGS

Note: To store, put the croquettes in an airtight container in a single layer and freeze. When you cook them, make sure that they are completely thawed.

Pine Nut-Crusted Chicken Breasts

Crunchy, creamy, and svelte all at once, cheese-stuffed, nut-crusted chicken breasts are a sybarite's dinner. Sissy gets her goat cheese from Vermont's own Does' Leap Farm and Boucher Farms.

Herbed Goat Cheese Stuffing

1	(11-ounce) log plain goat cheese
½	teaspoon dried oregano
½	teaspoon dried basil
2	garlic cloves, finely minced
1	shallot, finely minced
3	tablespoons rehydrated, chopped, sun-dried tomatoes
	Salt and pepper

Pine-Nut Crust

1	cup pine nuts
1	cup breadcrumbs
6	fresh basil leaves
1	garlic clove
	Salt and pepper

Chicken

6	(7-ounce) boneless skinless chicken breasts
1	egg
½	cup water
2	tablespoons olive or vegetable oil

Basil Cream Sauce

2	tablespoons butter
1	minced shallot
10	basil leaves, julienned
¼	cup white wine
2	cups heavy cream
	Salt and pepper

For the stuffing, in the bowl of an electric mixer with a paddle combine the goat cheese, oregano, basil, garlic, shallot, tomatoes, and salt and pepper to taste. Blend thoroughly.

For the crust, in a medium-size skillet over medium heat toast the pine nuts lightly until fragrant. In a food processor combine the pine nuts, breadcrumbs, basil, garlic, and salt and pepper to taste. Process until finely chopped and well combined.

For the chicken, preheat the oven to 350°F. Place each chicken breast on a cutting board. On the thicker side cut a horizontal slit in the breast to form a pocket. Place equal portions of the stuffing into each pocket and secure with a toothpick. Beat the egg and water together thoroughly. Dip each breast in the egg liquid and roll it in the pine-nut crust until evenly coated. Place a large skillet over medium heat and add the oil. When the oil begins to sizzle, brown the breasts on both sides and remove to a baking sheet or roasting pan. Place the breasts in the oven for 20 to 30 minutes or until cooked through.

While the chicken is cooking, prepare the basil cream sauce. Melt the butter in a one-quart saucepan over low heat. Add the shallot, basil, and white wine. Bring to a simmer and reduce the mixture for about 5 minutes. Add the heavy cream and reduce for another 5 minutes. Add salt and pepper to taste. When the chicken is done, remove it from the oven and serve with the basil cream sauce.

MAKES 6 SERVINGS

Turkey Burger

A great alternative to the classic hamburger," Sissy proclaims. It's great for those wanting to eat heart-healthy. And she notes that goat cheese adds a unique twist. She gets hers from either Consider Bardwell Farms or Does' Leap Farm in Vermont.

3	pounds ground turkey
1½	cups finely chopped red onion
¾	cup finely chopped fresh parsley
6	tablespoons plain yogurt
6	tablespoons goat cheese
2	tablespoons vegetable oil

Herbed Yogurt Sauce

2	cups yogurt
1	teaspoon fresh tarragon
2	teaspoons minced scallions
2	teaspoons julienned basil
2	teaspoons lemon juice

Preheat the oven to 350°F. In a large mixing bowl, using your hands, mix together the turkey, onion, parsley, and yogurt. Make the mixture into twelve patties. Place the crumbled goat cheese right in the center on the top of six patties. Then place the other patties on top to create six double-thick turkey burgers. Heat the oil in a large cast iron skillet over medium-high heat. Brown the patties quickly on both sides, and then transfer the skillet to the oven. Bake about 15 minutes. When you press down on the burger, the juice should run clear.

Prepare the Herbed Yogurt Sauce by combining the yogurt, tarragon, scallions, basil, and lemon juice in a mixing bowl. Stir until well mixed and serve with the Turkey Burgers.

MAKES 6 (8-OUNCE) BURGERS

PELTIER'S

Across the village green from the Dorset Inn is a white clapboard store called Peltier's. Centuries-old wood floors creak as customers help themselves to coffee in back and pick up Mrs. Murphy's cider donuts by the cash register. Quite possibly the oldest country store in America, Peltier's is a genuine antique that began in the early days of the Republic as a co-op where citizens paid ten dollars for the privilege of doing business, much of which was on the barter system.

It was first known as the Dorset Union Store, part of the New

England Protective Union, which provided members a system to keep track of inventory and receipts. Located in a building originally moved from the nearby town of Rupert, it had many owners and names through the 19th century. From 1894 to 1913, the town library was located on the second floor. In 1913 it was bought by John Peltier and Albert Chapman, the latter Dorset's postmaster. A soda fountain was added in 1926 (artifacts from which are now on display). Perry Peltier ran the store from the mid-1950s until 1977 when, at age 81, he sold it to Jay and Terry Hathaway, who in 2004 sold it to Ellen Stimson and John Rushing. The history-conscious Rushing-Stimson display countless antique kitchen implements, vintage photos, and the store's original ledger, in which the first entries date back to 1832. The upstairs store room still has the block-and-tackle wheel once used to hoist stock up and down.

Museum-like as it may be, Peltier's remains what it always has been —a country store with a welcoming feel for locals and tourists and an inventory that includes some of everything. There are gas pumps out front; DVDs and videos for rent inside, and an array of food that runs from fancy pasta and artisan breads to big jars of pickled eggs and fingerling sausages. One room is Peltier's Wine Shop; and of course there are shelves of maple products and Vermont cheeses galore. Recently, take-away dinners have been added to the repertoire; and up front, a glass case always contains at least a couple of Peltier's own pies, most notably a sweet-tart medley known as Fruits of the Forest.

Beef, Pork, Lamb & Game

Grilled Veal Chop with Prosciutto, Fontina, and Sage Butter

Roast Rack of Pork

Pork Schnitzel

Venison Stew

Pecan-Crusted Rack of Lamb with Balsamic Glaze

Beef Stroganoff

Braised Lamb Shanks

Sautéed Fresh Calf Liver

Glazed Corned Beef and Cabbage Dinner

Meatloaf

Shepherd's Pie

Grilled Veal Chops with Prosciutto, Fontina, and Sage Butter

The flavor combination of veal, proscuitto, fontina cheese, and sage is a jump-into-your-mouth classic, i.e. a variation on the traditional Roman dish saltimbocca.

Sage Butter		**Veal**	
1	pound butter, softened	6	veal chops, 1½-inches thick
4	shallots, minced		Vegetable oil
2	garlic cloves, minced		Salt and pepper
1	cup minced fresh sage	6	thin slices prosciutto
2	tablespoons minced parsley	6	thin slices fontina
1	teaspoon salt		
1	teaspoon pepper		

For the sage butter, soften the butter in the work bowl of an electric mixer or food processor. Add the shallots, garlic, sage, parsley, salt, and pepper. Mix together until incorporated and light in color.

For the veal, have your grill ready on medium heat. Brush each chop slightly with the oil on both sides. Salt and pepper the veal to taste. Grill about 8 minutes per side.

Preheat the oven to 350°F. Remove the veal chops from the grill and place them in a roasting pan. Top each chop with 1 teaspoon of the sage butter, then a slice of the prosciutto, and then a slice of the fontina. Place the pan in the oven just until the cheese melts. Serve with Tomato Coulis (see page 127).

MAKES 6 SERVINGS

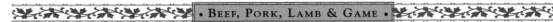

Roast Rack of Pork

Sissy uses gourmet, unspoiled pigs that are butchered locally at Over the Hill Farm. Dorset Inn chef Chris Burrows and his wife, Misse (who manages the front desk), recently began raising pigs on their farm. The pigs are fed compost from the kitchen as well as organic grain.

Stuffing

4	tablespoons butter
1	large onion
2	Granny Smith apples, sliced
½	cup roughly minced sage
	Salt and pepper

Pork and Sauce

2	tablespoons fresh sage, minced
2	shallots, minced
1	teaspoon garlic, minced
2	cups breadcrumbs
1	rack of pork, ask the butcher for a 6-rib rack or 1 to 2 ribs per serving
	Salt and pepper
	Vegetable oil
1	onion, chopped
1	carrot, chopped
2	celery ribs, chopped
½	plus ½ (750 ml) bottle white wine
1	cup cider
4	cups veal stock (see page 143)
4	tablespoons roux

For the stuffing, heat the butter in a sauté pan and add the onion, apple, sage, and salt and pepper to taste. Toss until the mixture is only slightly soft. Remove from the heat and allow to cool. It will cook further as the pork is roasted.

For the pork, combine the sage, shallots, garlic, and breadcrumbs. Open up the pork roast by carefully cutting along the bones. Sprinkle with the salt and pepper to taste. Spread the stuffing evenly in the pork and then close. Tie the pork between every other rib with cooking twine and brush the roast with a little oil.

Preheat the oven to 350°F. Sprinkle any remaining breadcrumb mixture all over the roast. Put the onion, carrot, and celery in the bottom of the roasting pan, and place the roast on top. Pour in half the bottle of wine, cover with aluminum foil, and bake for 1 hour. Covering with foil keeps the pork moist and the wine flavor penetrates the pork a little bit. Remove the foil and bake for 1 more hour. Add more wine as necessary. The pork will begin to color to a nice bronze. It should be very firm to the touch and just slightly pink. Transfer the pork to the serving platter.

For the sauce, carefully deglaze the roasting pan over low heat with the remaining half bottle of wine and cider, scraping up the brown bits on the bottom of the pan. Add the veal stock, bring to a boil, and stir until reduced by half (about 3 cups), approximately 10 minutes. Whisk in the roux. The sauce should thicken nicely. Put the sauce through a strainer, and serve it over the pork.

MAKES 6 SERVINGS

Pork Schnitzel

A fine alternative to veal. For these little schnitzels, Sissy uses the ends of the pork tenderloins. Home cooks can simply start with a whole pork tenderloin. Serve with scalloped potatoes and red cabbage.

12	small pieces pork tenderloin
1	cup all-purpose flour
2	eggs, beaten with a little water for an egg wash
2	cups seasoned breadcrumbs*
2	tablespoons vegetable oil
	Lemon juice
4	tablespoons capers
6	tablespoons white wine
½	cup chicken stock (see page 141)

Pound the pork between sheets of wax paper until ¼-inch thick. Dust each piece with flour and then dip it into the egg wash and dredge in the breadcrumbs. (This can be done in the morning and refrigerated.) Heat the oil in a sauté pan over medium heat. When hot, add the pieces of meat so they can cook evenly. When slightly browned on one side, turn over and cook the other side. As they cook, sprinkle the meat pieces with the lemon juice. As each piece is cooked, remove it to the serving platter. Add the capers, white wine, and chicken stock to the sauté pan and deglaze. Pour the sauce over the meat to serve.

MAKES 6 SERVINGS

Note: To season the breadcrumbs, mix 2 cups breadcrumbs with 1 teaspoon of the following herbs and spices: parsley, sage, thyme, salt, and pepper. (Or you can use Pepperidge Farm seasoned stuffing pulverized in the food processor.)

Venison Stew

We have a great may deer hunters around here," Sissy notes about this true New England dish. It is a stout autumn meal that is especially satisfying when served atop a bed of soft polenta (see page 167).

3	pounds venison stew meat
2	tablespoons sweet paprika
4	teaspoons dried thyme
2	teaspoons salt
2	teaspoons pepper
3	tablespoons vegetable oil
2	medium onions, coarsly chopped
4	garlic cloves, minced
2	carrots, peeled and sliced
2	celery ribs, thinly sliced
2	cups red wine
2	tablespoons all-purpose flour
2	(10-ounce) cans whole tomatoes, chopped
½	cup chicken stock (see page 141)

In a large mixing bowl, sprinkle the venison with the paprika, thyme, and salt and pepper to taste, and mix so that the meat is thoroughly covered. Heat the oil in a large sauté pan over medium heat. When the pan is hot, slowly add the venison. Brown the meat on all sides. Add the onions, garlic, carrots, and celery and stir for about 5 minutes. Add the red wine and deglaze the pan for about 5 minutes.

Preheat the oven to 350°F. After deglazing the pan, sprinkle the flour into the pan and stir. Add the tomatoes and chicken stock. The meat should be just covered with the liquid. If not, add a little more stock. Transfer the stew to a casserole dish and bake for 2 hours or until the meat is tender.

MAKES 12 SERVINGS

Pecan-Crusted Rack of Lamb with Balsamic Glaze

I try to use charro lamb when I can in this recipe," Sissy says. "It has such awesome flavor. The pecan crust and balsamic glaze complement each other and the lamb so well."

Balsamic Glaze

¾   cup balsamic vinegar

1½   cups heavy cream

1   teaspoon salt

Coating

1   cup pecan halves

½   cup panko (Japanese breadcrumbs)

1   garlic clove, minced

1   shallot, minced

       Salt and pepper

6   (4-bone) racks of lamb

For the glaze, in a small skillet reduce the vinegar to a paste over medium heat, about 8 minutes. Add the heavy cream, cook, and reduce for another 10 minutes until the mixture coats the back of a spoon. Add the salt.

Preheat the oven to 400°F. In a food processor combine the pecans, panko, garlic, shallot, and salt and pepper to taste, and process to an even consistency. Coat the racks with the pecan mixture. Place in a roasting pan and cook for about 15 minutes (for rare). Spoon some of the glaze onto each plate and place a rack of lamb on top.

MAKES 6 SERVINGS

Note: Great with oven-roasted new potatoes and a vegetable medley of roasted carrots, parsnips, and turnips.

Beef Stroganoff

Frugality is the principle behind Sissy's beef stroganoff, which is a good way to use the trimmings of a beef tenderloin. "Make sure the butcher gives them to you," she advises. "Or you can save them yourself if you clean your own tenderloin." Or, of course, it is possible to start from scratch using tender pieces of beef.

4	tablespoons vegetable oil
1	medium onion, diced
2	pounds sirloin or tenderloin pieces
2	teaspoons dried tarragon leaves
	Dash of Worcestershire sauce
2	teaspoons tomato paste
2	cups sour cream
	Salt and pepper

Heat the oil in a medium saucepan over medium heat. Add the onion and sauté until soft. Add the tenderloin and brown it, being careful not to let the onions burn. When the meat is browned, add the tarragon, Worcestershire sauce, tomato paste, and sour cream. Stir quickly and heat just until the sour cream is warm.

MAKES 6 TO 8 SERVINGS

Braised Lamb Shanks

E veryone's favorite," is how Sissy describes braised lamb shanks. "They look a little barbaric with the shank hanging out of the bowl, but they make a stupendous meal!" She suggests serving them with white beans. I try to use the native lamb shanks," Sissy says. "But when they are unavailable, I use Colorado lamb. They're a bit bigger than the natives."

2	tablespoons vegetable oil
6	lamb shanks
	Flour for dredging
	Salt and pepper
1	large white onion
6	garlic cloves, sliced
2	cups whole canned tomatoes, sliced
3	sprigs fresh oregano, chopped or 2 teaspoons dried
3	sprigs fresh thyme, chopped or 2 teaspoons dried
3	sprigs fresh rosemary, chopped or 2 teaspoons dried
8	cups veal stock (see page 143)

Heat the oil in a sauté pan. Dredge the shanks in flour, shake off the excess, and then salt and pepper them. Brown the lamb in the oil, being careful not to splatter yourself. Use long, sturdy tongs and perhaps turn down the heat a bit. You may have to brown in batches. Once a shank has browned evenly, place it in the roasting pan. Preheat the oven to 350°F. If the flour in the roasting pan is burnt, wipe the pan out with a paper towel. Then add about 4 more tablespoons oil to the pan, and over medium heat add the onions and garlic. Cook until soft. Then add the tomatoes, oregano, thyme, rosemary, and the veal stock and simmer for a few minutes. Taste for seasoning and add salt and pepper if necessary. Pour the sauce over the lamb shanks, cover with aluminum foil, and put in the oven for about 3 hours. The meat will begin to fall off the bones. Hold in a slow oven until ready to serve.

MAKES 6 SERVINGS

Sautéed Fresh Calf Liver

Fresh calf liver is the most popular item on the Dorset Inn menu. That is because Sissy's is the best in the world. She explains its popularity from a more modest perspective: "No two people in a family like calf liver, so it is hardly ever cooked at home." Thus, when liver-lovers dine at the inn, it is their opportunity to indulge.

6	plus 2 tablespoons vegetable oil or butter for sautéing
2	white onions, sliced
4	strips bacon, cooked crisp
6	slices fresh calf livers
	Salt and pepper
	Flour for dredging

Heat 2 tablespoons oil or butter in a sauté pan over medium heat. Sauté the onions until golden brown. Cook the bacon in a sauté pan or in the oven until crisp. Heat the remaining 6 tablespoons oil or butter in a medium sauté pan. Season the liver with salt and pepper to taste, and dredge the liver in the flour. When the pan is hot, shake the flour from the liver and place the liver in the pan. When browned on one side, quickly turn with tongs and brown the other side. This takes all of 5 minutes for rare, and another minute or 2 minutes on each side for more well done. Serve immediately with the onions and bacon.

MAKES 2 TO 3 SERVINGS

Glazed Corned Beef and Cabbage Dinner

My favorite dinner," Sissy declares. "The flavors are so varied but blend together so well. All you need is a little mustard, Grego's Irish soda bread, and a bottle of Guinness. . . . Then there's the corned beef hash you make with the leftovers!"

Brisket

5	pounds corned beef brisket
4	bay leaves
8	peppercorns
6	allspice berries
1	whole cinnamon stick
2	teaspoons mustard seed

Glaze

1	cup brown sugar
1	tablespoon dry mustard
¼	cup molasses
½	cup bourbon

Vegetables

6	medium red potatoes or 12 small
1	pound boiling onions
1	pound carrots, peeled and cut into sections
1	pound parsnips, peeled and cut into sections

1   *pound purple-top turnips, peeled and cut*
1   *pound beets*
1   *medium head cabbage, cut into 8 sections*
     Roux
     Parsley

Wash the brisket to remove any brine, and place it in a large kettle with the bay leaves, peppercorns, allspice berries, cinnamon stick, mustard seed, and enough water (about 24 cups) to cover. Bring this to a boil and simmer over moderate heat for about 1 hour per pound or until the center can be pierced easily with a pronged fork. Preheat the oven to 350°F.

To make the glaze, combine the brown sugar, dry mustard, molasses, and bourbon in a bowl. Remove the brisket to a roasting pan, reserving the broth. Put the brisket in the roasting pan fat side up. Spoon half the glaze over it and put it in the oven for about 30 minutes. Baste every 10 minutes with the remaining glaze until all is used. While the beef is glazing in the oven, begin cooking the vegetables in the reserved broth.

Bring the pot with the broth back to a boil. Reduce the heat to a simmer and drop in the red potatoes. Give them about a 5-minute head start. Add the onions and the carrots. Wait another 5 minutes and add the parsnips and turnips, and cook until everything is soft to the touch, approximately another 5 minutes. If the broth gets low, add some water. Make sure to cook the beets in a separate pot, because you don't want them to bleed into the other vegetables. When the vegetables are done, place them on a serving dish and cover to keep warm. Briefly cook the cabbage in the same broth for about 10 minutes and slice the corned beef. When the cabbage is done, arrange everything on a serving platter or use two platters. Strain the broth and add some roux to thicken for a sauce. Add the minced parsley for garnish.

MAKES 12 SERVINGS

Meatloaf

Meatloaf is on the menu every Tuesday at the Dorset Inn. One day a friend of Sissy's, Phyllis Brinkley, declared that her meatloaf is better than Sissy's, and that there should be a cook-off between the two of them to determine who makes the best. Sissy took the idea to kitchen outfitter J. K. Adams down the road, which instituted an annual meatloaf contest. Sissy is one of the judges, so she can't enter her meatloaf in the contest, and the face off between her and Phyllis has yet to happen.

1	pound ground beef
1	pound ground pork
1	pound ground veal
1	cup finely chopped onion
1	cup finely chopped green bell pepper
½	cup breadcrumbs
1	tablespoon horseradish
½	cup plus 6 tablespoons ketchup
4	eggs
2	tablespoons Worcestershire sauce
	Salt and pepper
3	slices bacon, each cut in half

Preheat the oven to 350°F. In a large bowl mix together the beef, pork, veal, onion, green bell pepper, breadcrumbs, horseradish, ½ cup ketchup, eggs, Worcestershire sauce, and salt and pepper to taste. Form the meat mixture into six individual loaves. Top each loaf with the remaining ketchup, 1 tablespoon per loaf, and a half slice of bacon. Place the loaves in a roasting pan with a little water in the bottom and bake for 30 minutes.

MAKES 6 SERVINGS

Shepherd's Pie

This is a great casserole for a dinner party. You can prepare it very simply or dress it up with additional vegetables.

2	pounds ground lamb
5	tablespoons vegetable oil
1	cup chopped onion
½	cup chopped turnips
⅓	cup chopped parsnips
1	cup chopped carrots
¼	cup chopped fresh herbs (rosemary, thyme, sage, oregano)
4	tablespoons butter
6	tablespoons all-purpose flour
3	cups veal or beef stock (see page 143)
	Salt and pepper
4	medium baking potatoes, peeled
1	egg
⅓	cup heavy cream
4	tablespoons butter

Preheat the oven to 350°F. In a large skillet brown the lamb in the olive oil over medium-high heat. Drain off most of the excess fat and move the lamb to a bowl. In the same skillet cook the onion, turnips, parsnips, and carrots until soft. Remove from the heat. Return the lamb to the pan along with the fresh herbs. In a small pan melt the butter over low heat and slowly stir in the flour until the roux is the consistency of wet sand. In a saucepan over medium heat bring the stock to a simmer. Whisk in the roux until the stock is as thick as gravy. Add the gravy to the lamb and vegetable mixture and season with the salt and pepper to taste. Put the mixture into a 2-quart casserole dish. Boil the potatoes until soft (35 to 45 minutes). Drain and mash with the egg, heavy cream, butter, and salt to taste. Spread the mashed potatoes over the meat mixture and bake for 30 minutes. For a nice brown crust, broil for 5 minutes.

MAKES 6 SERVINGS

NUNI RAGONESE

Nothing fazes Nuni Ragonese, who has been head waitress with Sissy at the Dorset Inn since the fall of 1986. "I once had someone drop dead in front of me," she recalled. "It was a heart attack. He was the bartender. It was the beginning of the dinner hour, so I took my little eighteen and nineteen-year-old waitresses and told them, 'We have ninety guests coming tonight. We must go on.'"

Nuni gave herself her unusual name when she was four years old because she felt the normal girl's name her mother had given her just didn't fit. Since childhood she has led life her own way. Her first job, when she was seventeen, was with an insurance company; but, she says, "I looked at too many blue skies out the window of my office. I thought, 'I have to get out of here.'" So she went up to Stratton to ski, and she never came back. She attributes her talents as a waitress to having worked at the Birken House at Stratton, where the proprietors, who were Austrian, were sticklers for hospitality. "I knew I liked Sissy right from the beginning," she remembers. "She takes being a chef seriously. Everything she does is for the customer. I don't care if it's a string bean, she wants it just right. No matter what happens in her personal life, hospitality comes first."

If you are lucky enough to have Nuni as a waitress, you will enjoy the privilege of hearing her describe dishes on the menu with enthusiasm that verges on food poetry. One evening at dinner we were wondering out loud about where to eat breakfast the next day. She insisted we return the next morning. She said we would find no corned beef hash anywhere that was more delicious than Sissy's. As usual, she was right.

Photo courtesy of Patrick Honan

Fish

&

Bouillabaisse

Fish 'n' Chips

Potato-Crusted Halibut

Baked Halibut

Grilled Tuna with Mango-Papaya Salsa

Sesame-Crusted Tuna

Macadamia-Crusted Swordfish Steaks

Coriander-Crusted Salmon

Pesto Crust for Monkfish

Pecan-Crusted Trout with a Lime-Parsley Butter

Bouillabaisse

The flavors of bouillabaisse blend together better if it is made a day in advance. Of course, it must be served with plenty of garlic toast so diners can sop up the delicious broth at the bottom of the bowl.

2	tablespoons vegetable oil	8	cups white wine
4	medium onions, sliced	8	cups water
2	leeks, julienned	2	(28-ounce) cans tomatoes
12	garlic cloves, crushed	4	(1¼-pound) cooked lobsters
4	sprigs saffron	1	pound monkfish, cubed
10	sprigs thyme	1	pound shrimp
1	teaspoon red pepper flakes	½	pound scallops
2	bay leaves	2	pounds mussels, cleaned
4	teaspoons salt		

Heat the oil in a large pot, and sauté the onions, leeks, garlic, saffron, thyme, red pepper flakes, bay leaves, and salt until the vegetables are soft. Add the wine and water and bring to a boil. Simmer covered for 30 minutes. Then add the tomatoes with their juice. With the broth at a simmer, add the monkfish. About 5 minutes later, add the shrimp, scallops, and mussels. When these are almost cooked, about 3 minutes, add the lobster meat. Cook until the fish and mussels are cooked through and the lobster is warm. The mussels will open when they are cooked; discard any that do not. Serve with garlic toast.

MAKES 8 SERVINGS

Fish 'n' Chips

"This reminds me of my stay in Scotland where you can go to the fish-n-chip stands in the streets," Sissy says. "They hand you wax paper filled with the freshly fried fish-n-chips and a side of malt vinegar—messy, but fun. I have modified the tradition to a sit-down meal in the tavern or the dining room."

Batter

1½	cups all-purpose flour
¼	teaspoon garlic powder
¼	teaspoon onion powder
1	teaspoon baking powder
1	beer, Michelob or an ale, whatever you prefer
	Salt and pepper

4	cups canola oil for frying
6	(6-ounce) haddock or cod fillets
	Old Bay Seasoning (available in specialty, and some grocery, stores)

For the batter, combine in a mixing bowl the flour, garlic powder, onion powder, baking powder, beer, and salt and pepper to taste and mix well.

Heat the oil in a deep frying pan until a drop of water dripped into the oil sizzles. Sprinkle the fish with the Old Bay Seasoning. Take one fillet at a time, cover with the batter, and carefully drop it into the oil. Cook the fillets for about 5 minutes. Serve with the chips.

MAKES 6 SERVINGS

A pleasant spring day in Dorset, Vermont. "Breakfast" is missing from the sign only because the sign-painter didn't have room for it.

The front desk in the Dorset Inn is usually "manned" by the Inn's unofficial greeters, Anise and Aggie, chef Sissy Hicks' Labrador retriever and basset hound.

Maple syrup is good, but nothing beats local blueberries for topping a plate of waffles.

Omelets are made from eggs so fresh that they cackle when the chef cracks them.

A reading nook on the ground floor of America's oldest continuously operated inn

Corned beef hash (page 39) is always well complemented by a couple of fried eggs on top.

Pancakes (page 4) and sausage patties topped with pure Vermont maple syrup

French toast (page 3) and bacon dusted with powdered sugar

*Chicken salad (page 64)
surrounded by a phalanx of
garden-fresh tomato wedges*

*A grilled sandwich with focaccia
bread, still too warm to eat*

*On the road to Dorset you can find out
what time it is by studying this sundial
on the side of a barn.*

Comfort food extraordinaire: Dorset Inn rarebit

Barbecued chicken sided by long wedges of luscious sweet potato

Sissy squeezes juice from her low-tech appliance known as "Big Orange."

An appetizer made from a festival of local mushrooms

The richest, most luxurious garlic bread (page 42) you will ever eat

Eggplant crêpes, topped with melted cheese

Braised lamb shank (page 102):
one of Chef Sissy's favorites

A New England favorite: fish and
chips (page 112)

Sesame tuna (page 116) topped with wilted greens

Bread pudding (page 197) in a pool of bourbon sauce

Rhubarb pie (page 187)—a la mode, of course.

Sissy's homemade profiteroles

Chef Sissy Hicks at the stove

Potato-Crusted Halibut

Sissy advises that making Potato-Crusted Halibut is easier than it might seem at first. The most important advice she has is to keep the potatoes covered with water or lemon juice as they are peeled or grated. That insures they won't turn brown.

5	Idaho potatoes
½	cup lemon juice
½	cup heavy cream
	Minced dill
	Salt and pepper
3	teaspoons Old Bay seasoning
6	(6-ounce) halibut fillets
	Flour for dredging
2	tablespoons vegetable oil

Peel the potatoes and put them in cold water. Put the lemon juice in a medium-size mixing bowl. Coarsely grate the potatoes into the lemon juice. Keep tossing the potatoes in the juice as you add them. This keeps the potatoes from turning brown. When all the potatoes are grated, add the heavy cream, dill, salt, and pepper. You should have a thick, not too milky, mixture. Sprinkle the fillets with some Old Bay Seasoning and dredge lightly in the flour. Hold the fillet in one hand and pat the grated potato mixture on evenly until the whole fillet is coated. Place on parchment paper on a plate. Continue until all the fillets are coated.

When ready to cook, preheat the oven to 400°F, and heat the oil in a sauté pan. Place 2 fillets at a time into the oil. Fry until nicely browned and crisp. Flip over and brown the other side. Place in a roasting pan. Continue this procedure until all the pieces are crispy on both sides, but not completely cooked. Put the roasting pan in the oven for 10 minutes or until cooked through.

MAKES 6 SERVINGS

Baked Halibut

This recipe works equally well if shrimp are substituted for halibut and the shrimp are served on a bed of angel hair pasta with garlic toast on the side.

2	tablespoons vegetable oil
¼	cup minced fresh ginger
5	garlic cloves, minced
4	shallots, minced
½	leek, sliced, white part only
	Salt and pepper
1	bay leaf
2	sprigs fresh thyme
½	teaspoon crushed red pepper flakes
4	cups white wine
4	cups water
1	(28-ounce) can whole tomatoes, chopped, not drained
6	(6-ounce) halibut fillets
	Mashed potatoes or spinach

Preheat the oven to 350°F. Heat the oil in a medium saucepan over medium heat, and sauté the ginger, garlic, shallots, and leek until softened. Add the salt, pepper, bay leaf, thyme, and pepper flakes. Stir in the wine, water, and tomatoes and simmer for about 30 minutes. Remove the bay leaf. Place the halibut in an ovenproof dish and cover with some of the tomato broth. Bake this in the oven for 15 to 20 minutes or until the fish is firm to the touch. In a serving bowl, lay the halibut fillets on a bed of mashed potatoes and spinach and spoon the leftover broth over the top.

MAKES 6 SERVINGS

Grilled Tuna with Mango-Papaya Salsa

An alternative to marinating tuna is to blacken it using Emeril's blackening mix. The sweet salsa is a vivid contrast to the blackening spice.

Marinade		**Mango-Papaya Salsa**	
½	cup olive oil	1	mango, peeled and pitted
2	shallots, minced	1	papaya, peeled and seeded
2	tablespoons minced fresh cilantro	1	shallot, minced
			Juice of 3 limes, approximately ¼ cup
	Salt and pepper	¼	cup cilantro, minced
2	garlic cloves , minced	1	tablespoon fresh ginger, minced
2	tablespoons lime juice		Salt and pepper
¼	cup Dijon mustard		
6	(6-ounce) tuna steaks		

To prepare the tuna, combine the oil, shallots, cilantro, salt and pepper, garlic, lime juice, and mustard. Pour over the tuna and marinate for 1 to 2 hours.

Prepare the Mango-Papaya Salsa. Dice the mango and papaya and combine with the shallot, lime juice, cilantro, ginger, and salt and pepper to taste. Let it sit at room temperature for about 1 hour before serving, giving the flavors a chance to meld.

When ready to cook, remove the tuna from the marinade and place on a lightly oiled grill. Cook over medium heat 5 to 6 minutes on each side. Serve hot with the relish spooned over the top.

MAKES 6 SERVINGS

Sesame-Crusted Tuna

Wasabi is Japanese horseradish, and it is usually sinus-clearingly hot. You can buy it in tubes at specialty food shops and Japanese grocery stores.

2	tablespoons wasabi powder	2	cups sesame seeds
¼	cup plus 2 tablespoons water	½	cup all-purpose flour
6	(6-ounce) tuna steaks	1	tablespoon fresh cilantro
2	eggs	1	garlic clove, minced
1	teaspoon lemon juice	2	tablespoons toasted sesame oil
	Salt and pepper		

Make a paste of the wasabi powder and 2 tablespoons water. To prepare the tuna steaks, spread ½ teaspoon paste on each tuna steak; one side is sufficient. Whisk the eggs with the remaining ¼ cup water, lemon juice, and salt and pepper to taste in a mixing bowl. To make the crust, put the sesame seeds, flour, cilantro, and garlic in a food processor and process until the sesame seeds are finely ground, 2 to 3 minutes. Put the sesame mixture on a plate. Coat the tuna by dipping each piece carefully into the egg mixture. Let the excess drip off and then place on the plate with the sesame flour, dredging both sides. Put the tuna on parchment paper or another dish until ready to use.

When ready to cook, preheat the oven to 450°F. Heat the sesame oil in a medium-size sauté pan on medium-high heat. When hot, carefully brown the tuna on one side for about 30 seconds. It should be nice and brown but not burnt. Turn the tuna over and brown quickly on the other side. Put in a roasting pan and place in the oven for about 5 minutes for medium rare or a little longer for medium doneness.

MAKES 6 SERVINGS

Note: With very fresh tuna, you want to eat it sushi-style, nice and rare. I serve it with Wasabi Butter (see page 136) and a side of Citrus Soy Sauce (see page 140).

Macadamia-Crusted Swordfish Steaks

A mighty, meaty seafood meal, nicely abetted by roasted red pepper sauce.

1	cup macadamia nuts
½	cup all-purpose flour
	Salt and pepper
1	teaspoon ginger
1	garlic clove, minced
2	teaspoons minced cilantro
2	eggs
½	cup water
1	teaspoon lemon juice
6	(6-ounce) swordfish steaks (ask for thick ones)
2	tablespoons vegetable oil

To prepare the crust, process the nuts, flour, salt, pepper, ginger, garlic, and cilantro in a food processor until the mixture resembles ground breadcrumbs. Place the mixture in a small pan so you can coat the swordfish easily. In another small bowl, combine the eggs, water, and lemon juice. Dip the swordfish into the egg wash and then coat on all sides with the macadamia nut mixture. (This can be done ahead of time; then place the fish between waxed paper and store in the refrigerator).

Preheat the oven to 400°F. Heat the oil in a sauté pan. You can do two steaks at a time. Brown on one side for about 2 minutes, and then carefully turn over with a spatula and brown 2 minutes on the other side. Put the steaks in a roasting pan. When all the pieces are browned, put the roasting pan in the oven for about 8 minutes. Using a knife, check to see if they are cooked through. This is great with Roasted Red Pepper Sauce on page 139.

MAKES 6 SERVINGS

DORSET'S MOST FAMOUS ANONYMOUS SON

The best-known person from Dorset was publicly nameless until after he died. Bill Wilson, cofounder of Alcoholics Anonymous, was born in East Dorset, just the other side of Mt. Aeolus from Dorset Village. His birthplace, built in 1852 and originally called the Mt. Aeolus Inn, was a halfway-station between New York and Montreal for travelers along Route 7. It was run by his grandmother and called the Wilson House when he came into the world in 1895. In the 1930s when Prohibition ended, new owners made a bar out of his birth room. Later in life, after becoming sober and creating the program that has helped millions of others achieve sobriety, Wilson would joke that he was born in the back of a barroom.

In her biography, *My Name is Bill*, Susan Cheever points out that the principles of AA are derived to a large degree from the Vermont upbringing of Bill Wilson (and Bob Smith, AA cofounder and fellow Vermonter). The idea of everyone's voice being equal and everyone's opinion being welcome (as is true of AA meetings) comes from the town meetings that were the foundation of democracy in Vermont (town meetings which, by the way, were frequently held in the town tavern). Cheever also points out that much of the state was dry when Wilson grew up and that temperance was a subject taught in schools. She calls Vermont a place where "self-righteousness about not drinking lived side by side with self-righteousness about drinking anyway." Furthermore, at the turn of the century when Wilson was born, this part of the Northeast was rife with the sort of transcendental searching that was so essential to his belief that real sobriety was based on a spiritual awakening.

Wilson, his sister, Dorothy, and mother, Emily, sometimes camped at nearby Emerald Lake (a.k.a. North Dorset Pond), named because its water glistens green from marble-quarry run-off. It was there that he met and courted Lois Burnham, whose well-to-do Brooklyn family had a summer cottage in the area. In September 1915 Bill proposed to Lois at the Lake, and they became secretly engaged.

The Wilson House remained a hostelry into the 1970s, when its doors were shuttered. Then in 1987 new owners began a major restoration. Now operating as a nonprofit foundation, the Wilson House has fourteen guest rooms as well as a meeting room for members of AA and other Twelve-Step recovery programs. In 1995 the Wilson House was listed on the National Register of Historic Places.

After he died in 1971, Bill Wilson was buried in the East Dorset Community Cemetery. His grave has become a compelling attraction for tourists whose lives have been transformed by the program he cofounded. It is not uncommon to visit the grave and find it strewn with AA coins, the silver-dollar-size medallions that recovering alcoholics earn for extended periods of sobriety. People leave their coins here as a token of thanks to the East Dorset man who blazed a path that led them out of addiction.

Coriander-Crusted Salmon

A salmon dish with a great melody of flavors, this is especially good when combined with citrus salsa.

2	cups panko (Japanese breadcrumbs)	**Citrus Salsa**	
1	tablespoon coriander seed	2	ruby red grapefruit, peeled and sectioned
2	teaspoons ground coriander	4	navel oranges, peeled and sectioned
	Salt and pepper	2	kiwifruit, peeled and sliced
	Zest of 1 lemon	½	red pepper, julienned
2	tablespoons minced parsley	¼	cup minced cilantro
6	salmon fillets	½	cup fresh lime juice
4	tablespoons butter	¼	cup honey
		1	piece fresh ginger, peeled and minced

Preheat the oven to 350°F. Put the panko, coriander seed, ground coriander, salt and pepper to taste, lemon zest, and parsley in the work bowl of a food processor and pulse until fine. Dredge the salmon fillets in the breadcrumb mixture. In a large saucepan heat the butter over medium heat. Brown the salmon in the butter, about 5 minutes per side. You may have to do this in batches. Transfer the fillets to a baking sheet and bake in the oven for about 10 minutes.

Prepare the Citrus Salsa. In a large stainless mixing bowl combine the grapefruit, oranges, kiwifruit, red pepper, cilantro, lime juice, honey, and ginger. Serve hot or cold. Serve the salmon over sautéed spinach with the Citrus Salsa.

MAKES 6 SERVINGS

Pesto Crust for Monkfish

This crust is especially good for stout, meaty fish. At the Dorset Inn you will find it jacketing big, moist hunks of monkfish.

2	cups panko (Japanese breadcrumbs)
2	garlic cloves
¼	cup pine nuts
½	cup fresh basil leaves
	Salt and pepper
3	pounds monkfish
4	tablespoons butter

In a food processor combine the panko, garlic, pine nuts, basil, and salt and pepper to taste. Process until well mixed to a very fine texture. Slice the monkfish diagonally into 6 pieces. Dredge each fillet in the pesto crust. In a large saucepan over medium heat, melt the butter. When hot, brown the monkfish fillets on both sides, about 5 minutes per side. You may have to do this in batches. Keep the cooked fillets warm in a 200°F-oven while cooking the remaining fillets. Serve with couscous and Mediterranean Salsa (see page 19).

MAKES 6 SERVINGS

Pecan-Crusted Trout with Lime-Parsley Butter

Sissy notes, "Trout and pecans may sound like a strange combination, but the nuts enhance the flavor of the trout. I serve this with mashed potatoes and sautéed spinach."

2	cups pecans		**Lime-Parsley Butter**
1	cup all-purpose flour		Zest and juice of 1 lime
3	eggs	1	shallot, minced
2	tablespoons lime juice	½	cup minced fresh parsley, chives, or dill
2	tablespoons cold water		
	Salt and pepper	½	pound (2 sticks) unsalted butter at room temperature
6	(8-ounce) skinless trout fillets		Salt and pepper
2	tablespoons clarified butter, more if needed		
6	tablespoons butter for frying		

Purée the pecans and flour to a fine powder in a food processor. Whisk the eggs, lime juice, water, and salt and pepper to taste until combined. Add the trout fillets to the egg mixture, turning to coat on each side. Cover and chill for 1 hour.

For the lime-parsley butter, in a medium-size bowl combine the lime zest and juice, shallot, parsley, butter, and salt and pepper to taste. Using a whisk, or stand mixer, whip until soft.

Remove the trout from the refrigerator and coat with the pecan flour on each side. Shake off the excess. Heat the butter in a skillet over medium-high heat. Fry the trout fillets in batches, 3 minutes per side, or until firm and golden brown. Sprinkle with the lime juice while sautéing. Top with the Lime-Parsley Butter.

MAKES 6 SERVINGS

Sauces

Aïoli

Tomato Sauce

Tomato Coulis

Hollandaise

Béarnaise

Basil-Tomato Brown Sauce

Tapenade

Madeira Sauce

Wasabi Butter

Plum Chutney

James Beard Steak Butter

Roasted Red Pepper Sauce

Citrus Soy Sauce

Chicken Stock

Vegetable Stock

Veal Stock

Duck Stock

Tomato-Cucumber Relish

Aïoli

A wonderful garlicky mayonnaise, roasted red pepper aïoli (rouille) is especially good on the Melbas served with steamed shrimp in ginger-garlic-tomato broth; and both the rouille and dill aïoli are suggested as a condiment for grilled fish or a swordfish sandwich or even a grilled vegetable sandwich.

6	garlic cloves
2	teaspoons Dijon mustard
4	egg yolks
2	teaspoons lemon juice
	Salt and pepper
1½	cups olive oil

Combine the garlic, mustard, egg yolks, lemon juice, and salt and pepper to taste in a food processor. With the motor running, add the oil very slowly, until a mayonnaise is formed.

MAKES ABOUT 2 CUPS

Note: There are several variations to the basic aïoli. For a rouille—a roasted red pepper aïoli—add one roasted red pepper peeled and seeded to the other ingredients in the food processor and blend before adding the oil. For a basil aïoli, add 1 cup fresh basil leaves. For a dill aïoli, add 1 cup fresh dill.

Tomato Sauce

To transform this tomato sauce into something well-suited for topping pasta, add mussels, shrimp, and scallops.

2	tablespoons vegetable oil
1	onion, diced
2	celery ribs, diced
1	green pepper, diced
1	carrot, diced
1	tablespoon minced garlic
1	small (2-ounce) can anchovies
2	teaspoons dried oregano
2	teaspoons dried basil
2	whole bay leaves
2	teaspoons salt
1	teaspoon black pepper
2	(28-ounce) cans whole tomatoes
2	cups water

Heat the oil in a medium-size stainless steel pot. Add the onion, celery, green pepper, carrot, garlic, and anchovies and cook for about 5 minutes. Add the oregano, basil, bay leaves, salt, and pepper and cook for another 5 minutes. The vegetables should be coated and just slightly wilted. Add the tomatoes and the water. Let simmer for about 30 minutes and remove from the heat. Purée in a food processor, but not too finely, and then let cool.

MAKES 4 CUPS

Tomato Coulis

Mushrooms and Madeira sauce give this a woody, earthy flavor. It's a great accompaniment for grilled meats such as veal chops or grilled polenta.

2	tablespoons unsalted butter
½	small onion, thinly sliced
6	shiitake mushrooms, thinly sliced
2	shallots, thinly sliced
1	small leek, white part only, thinly sliced
¼	teaspoon salt
2	tablespoons brandy
½	cup Madeira Sauce (see page 132)
1	cup chicken stock
6	ripe tomatoes with skins, chopped
2	sprigs thyme, chopped
1	bay leaf
	Salt and pepper

Melt 2 tablespoons butter in a medium-size skillet over low heat. Add the onion, mushrooms, shallots, leek, and salt and sauté until soft, about 7 minutes. Add the brandy and Madeira Sauce. Turn the heat to high and light the brandy with a match. Be careful of the flame. Simmer until the liquid is reduced by half. Add the chicken stock, tomatoes, thyme, and bay leaf. Reduce the heat to low and simmer uncovered for 15 minutes. Pulse the stock mixture in the food processor until just roughly chopped.

MAKES ABOUT 4 CUPS

Hollandaise

There are several versions of Hollandaise," Sissy notes. "It is a simple combination of butter, egg yolks, and lemon juice whisked over low, low heat with the clarified butter added very slowly." Hollandaise is necessary for eggs benedict and is a fine complement to potato pancakes or any grilled fish or vegetables.

4	egg yolks
½	teaspoon salt
¼	teaspoon cayenne
1	tablespoon water
2	teaspoons lemon juice, or less depending on taste
2	sticks butter, clarified, at room temperature

Place the egg yolks, salt, cayenne, water, and lemon juice in a mixing bowl with a rounded bottom (easier to whisk). Whisk the mixture over very low heat until it thickens like a pudding. It will turn very light in color. Remove from the heat. Slowly add the clarified butter, whisking constantly until all the butter is added. The sauce will become thick and light with a lovely lemon flavor.

MAKES ABOUT 2 CUPS

Note: Hollandaise will hold at room temperature for about a half hour.

Béarnaise

Béarnaise is traditionally served alongside tenderloin of beef; it's a good companion also for grilled swordfish or grilled chicken breast and is wonderful with roast beaf hash for breakfast or brunch.

Béarnaise Base

1	shallot, chopped
1	tablespoon minced fresh tarragon
1	cup tarragon vinegar
1	cup red wine
½	cup water

Sauce

4	egg yolks
½	teaspoon salt

¼	teaspoon cayenne
1	tablespoon water
2	teaspoons béarnaise base
2	sticks butter, clarified, at room temperature
1	tablespoon minced fresh tarragon
1	tablespoon minced tomato
	Pinch of dried parsley
	Pinch of ground black pepper

For the base, combine the shallot, tarragon, tarragon vinegar, red wine, and water in a small saucepan. Simmer until reduced by half, then strain. This keeps in the refrigerator indefinitely.

Place the egg yolks, salt, cayenne, water, and béarnaise base in a mixing bowl with a rounded bottom (easier to whisk). Over very low heat whisk until it thickens, like a pudding. It turns very light in color. Remove from the heat. Slowly add the clarified butter, whisking constantly until all the butter is added. It will be very light and thick. Fold in the tarragon, tomato, parsley, and pepper. Continue whisking until the sauce becomes thick.

MAKES 2 CUPS

Note: This sauce will hold at room temperature for half an hour.

Basil-Tomato Brown Sauce

When basil is fresh and tomatoes are ripening on the vine, this sauce is a great way to take full advantage of summer's flavors. It is great with Grilled Veal Chops (see page 95) or grilled lamb chops.

2	tablespoons vegetalbe oil
2	shallots, julienned
1	garlic clove, minced
1	cup basil, julienned
1	cup white wine
1	plum tomato, diced
4	cups veal stock (see page 143)
	Roux, if necessary

Heat the oil in a saucepan over medium heat and lightly sauté the shallots and garlic. Add the basil and white wine, bring to a boil, and reduce by half. Add the tomato and stock and reduce for about 15 minutes until thick. If it does not thicken, whisk in a tablespoon of roux. Pour the sauce into a container and cool to room temperature. It will keep for up to one week in the refrigerator and can be frozen in small containers or in ice cube trays.

MAKES 6 CUPS

Tapenade

Tapenade has dozens of uses. Sissy suggests spreading it on Melbas with goat cheese or tossing it with green beans as a vegetable side dish. It's also good with chicken liver pâte or grilled swordfish.

1	cup kalamata olives, pitted
2	garlic cloves
8	anchovy fillets
1	tablespoon capers
1	tablespoon minced parsley
½	cup olive oil

Finely mince the olives, garlic, anchovy fillets, and capers. Combine in a mixing bowl with the parsley. Add the oil, whisking until blended.

MAKES ABOUT 2 CUPS

Madeira Sauce

Rich and mahogany red, this sauce is Sissy's favorite complement for sautéed chicken livers. It's also good with veal scallops.

2	shallots, julienned
1	tablespoon minced tarragon
1	cup sliced shiitake mushrooms
2	tablespoons butter
1	cup Madeira
1	tomato, diced
4	cups veal stock (see page 143)
2	tablespoons roux

Sauté the shallots, tarragon, and mushrooms in the butter until softened. Deglaze the pan with the Madeira, and add the tomato and stock. Cook until slightly reduced. Slowly whisk in the roux and simmer for about 10 minutes or until thickened. Pour into a container and let cool to room temperature. This sauce can be frozen in small containers or ice cube trays.

MAKES 6 CUPS

GREEN MOUNTAIN BOYS

The place called Vermont originally belonged to France—hence its name, derived from the French words Mont Vert (green mountain)—but it was won by the British in 1763 during the French and Indian War. Two years earlier, New Hampshire Governor Wentworth had begun chartering towns in the unpopulated no-man's-land between the Connecticut River and a line twenty miles east of the Hudson. While New York's Governor Clinton protested—believing this region to be his domain—he was content to leave the matter of who owned the Green Mountain territory for King George to settle. Between 1761 and 1775 Wentworth chartered 128 towns. In an effort to get the king on his side, these New Hampshire "Grants," as they were termed, were named to flatter royal friends, including Lionel Cranfield Sackville, the first earl of Dorset.

Dorset was an especially confusing entity, a hollow defined by surrounding mountains: Mother Myrick to the southwest, Mt. Aeolus (sometimes called Dorset Mountain) to the south, and the Dorset-Danby Ridge to the east. Dorset, South Dorset, East Dorset, and North Dorset each have their own geographical character—all close together, yet separated by topography.

By the mid-1760s, New York's government was becoming exasperated with Wentworth's blithe appropriation of land for his New Hampshire Grants. Then-acting New York Governor Colden announced that his state's jurisdiction extended all the way to the Connecticut River. Colden's proclamation marked the beginning of a decade of popular resistance in the Grants against the authority of New York, which was seen by the independent-minded settlers as a colony of arrogant land barons. In 1769, two years after the charter of Dorset, Ethan Allen, whose family was from Dorset, arose as the leader of the Green Mountain Boys, an irregular militia consisting of his brothers, cousins, and a few hundred neighbors all set on resisting the hegemony of New York.

Based in the Catamount Tavern in Bennington, the Green Mountain Boys did what they had to do to prevent New York authorities and surveyors from intruding on what they considered their land. Their weapons ranged from broadside propaganda to flintlock rifles; while author Susan Cheever writes that Ethan Allen was "a young man who might in another state and another time be classified as a juvenile delinquent," his fiery will to fight for what was right made him a significant player in the birth of the United States and of the state of Vermont.

In 1774 the New York legislature passed an act designed to squash the "spirit of licentiousness" that had taken over in the land west of the Green Mountains, specifically identifying Ethan Allen as a main troublemaker. In response to this Riotous Assemblies Act, the first Dorset Convention of 1775 pledged self-defense. An open letter from the Green Mountain Boys expressed their stand in no uncertain terms: "We will kill and destroy any person or persons whomsoever, that shall presume to be accessory, aiding or assisting in taking any of us."

In May, two weeks after the Battle of Lexington and the start of the American Revolution, Ethan Allen and the Green Mountain Boys assembled on the Dorset Green. Together with General Benedict Arnold and his troops, they marched on the vital military position of Fort Ticonderoga and captured it. Allen and his boys snuck into the fort at night and roused the sleeping British commander at dawn, May 10, 1775. "The captain came immediately to the door with his breeches in his hand," Allen recalled. "I ordered him to deliver me the fort instantly."

The Continental Congress rewarded Allen for taking Ticonderoga and commended the Green Mountain Boys for their strategic victory. It looked to be the beginning of a brilliant military career for the young man. In 1775, however, while trying to take the city of Montreal, Allen was captured by the enemy and held prisoner for two years.

With a War of Independence igniting, New York's persecution of the riotous settlers of the New Hampshire Grants waned; and by the time of the Fourth Dorset Convention in September 1776, delegates declared themselves a separate district, beholden neither to New York nor New Hampshire, and free of Britain's tyranny, too. The next year, delegates proclaimed the New Hampshire Grants "a Separate Free and Independent jurisdiction or State by the name to be forever hereafter called and known and distinguished by the name of New Connecticut, alias Vermont."

After 1776 Vermont was the Republic of Vermont; and despite its not being one of the thirteen colonies, its role in the Revolutionary War was critical. In August 1777, as the British under General Burgoyne came south from Quebec in an attempt to isolate New England from the rest of the colonies, the Yankees took a stand on a hillside just over the border in Walloomsac, New York. The redcoats and their Hessian mercenaries had assumed local citizens would supply them with fresh horses and supplies, but instead, they were met by unyielding militia units from Vermont, New Hampshire, and western Massachusetts under the command of Gen. John Stark. The three-hour Battle of Bennington was a resounding victory for the Patriots, and the beginning of the end for Burgoyne, who surrendered two months later at Saratoga.

In 1791 Vermont joined the Union—the fourteenth state, and the first colony to become part of the new nation after the War of Independence.

Wasabi Butter

The punch of wasabi makes this butter especially welcome with rich-flavored fish such as tuna, yellowtail, or swordfish.

16	tablespoons (2 sticks) butter, softened
1	shallot, minced
1	tablespoon cilantro, minced
¼	cup wasabi paste
½	teaspoon salt
½	teaspoon pepper

Put the softened butter in a mixing bowl of an electric mixer with the paddle extension. Then add the shallot, cilantro, wasabi paste, salt, and pepper. Mix for about 5 minutes. Store the mixture in a container in the refrigerator.

MAKES 1½ CUPS

Plum Chutney

Dark and sweet and a little bit smoky-hot, plum chutney is the essential companion to Duck Confit (see page 81).

2	pounds plums, pitted and coarsely chopped
1	cup Granny Smith apples, not peeled, cored, and chopped
1	cup sliced onion
½	cup raisins
½	cup grated carrot
1	cup packed brown sugar
1	cup white vinegar
1	cup raspberry vinegar
1	tablespoon salt
1	teaspoon ground cloves
1	teaspoon ground ginger (or fresh, minced)
1	teaspoon allspice
1	chipotle chile pepper, seeded and diced

Mix the plums, apples, onion, raisins, carrot, and brown sugar in a large mixing bowl. Heat the vinegars, salt, cloves, ginger, allspice, and chile pepper in a large pot over medium heat. Bring to a boil. Add the plum mixture and bring back to a boil. Reduce the heat and simmer for a few hours, stirring every now and then until thickened. Remove from the heat and cool. This will thicken further upon standing. The chutney can be stored in the refrigerator for a couple of weeks.

MAKES ABOUT 1½ QUARTS

James Beard Steak Butter

At the beginning of my career I read James Beard and Julia Child, "Sissy recalls. "I remember when grilling a steak James would top it with a little butter, garlic, mustard, and a dash of Worcestershire sauce. I made this into a butter that is great on grilled steaks."

32	tablespoons (4 sticks) butter, softened
6	garlic cloves, minced
4	dashes Worcestershire sauce
5	tablespoons Dijon mustard
5	tablespoons puréed tomato
	Salt and pepper
	Pinch of paprika

Combine the butter, garlic, Worcestershire sauce, mustard, tomato, salt and pepper to taste, and a pinch of paprika into a stand mixer. With the paddle attachment mix for about 5 minutes. This can be stored in the refrigerator or frozen.

MAKES ABOUT 2 CUPS

Roasted Red Pepper Sauce

The end of the summer growing season means an abundance of fresh vegetables, especially peppers. That's the time to process them into this very versatile sauce. This can be served cold on a vegetable burger or hot with Potato-Crusted Halibut (see page 113).

3	red bell peppers, roasted, peeled, and seeded
1	teaspoon minced garlic
1	tablespoon balsamic vinegar
1	teaspoon grated fresh ginger
1	teaspoon salt
	Pinch of cayenne
5	dashes Tabasco
3	tablespoons tomato sauce
¼	teaspoon black pepper
3	tablespoons olive oil

Combine the peppers, garlic, vinegar, ginger, salt, cayenne, Tabasco, tomato sauce, black pepper, and olive oil in a food processor. Process until smooth, about 5 minutes. This can be stored in the refrigerator or frozen.

MAKES ABOUT 1½ CUPS

Citrus Soy Sauce

The slightly citrus flavor of this sauce makes it great with sesame tuna.

2	cups low-sodium soy sauce
1	cup orange juice
¼	cup lime juice
¼	leek, sliced
2	tablespoons minced fresh ginger
1	shallot, sliced
½	cup grapefruit juice
	Small amounts of the orange, lime, and grapefruit rinds (¾-inch peels)
½	cup rice wine vinegar

Combine the soy sauce, orange juice, lime juice, leek, ginger, shallot, grapefruit juice, the rinds, and vinegar in a stainless steel pot and bring to a boil. Reduce the heat and simmer for about 5 minutes. Cool and strain. This will keep in the refrigerator for a couple of weeks.

MAKES ABOUT 4 CUPS

Chicken Stock

Of course, you can buy chicken stock at the grocery store, but making your own is easy . . . and the result tends to be ever so much more delicious.

2	*pounds chicken bones*
2	*celery ribs*
1	*carrot*
1	*small onion*
	Several black peppercorns
1	*garlic head, halved*
	Sprigs of thyme, tarragon, and parsley

Combine the chicken bones, celery, carrot, onion, peppercorns, garlic, and herb sprigs in a large pot and cover with cold water. Bring the mixture to a boil, reduce the heat to simmer, and cook for 1 to 2 hours. Strain the stock into a container, cool, and refrigerate until ready to use. Discard the vegetables.

MAKES ABOUT 2 QUARTS

Note: You can freeze the stock in small containers or ice cube trays, allowing you to use what you need at a later time.

Vegetable Stock

For those who want to make soups and stews with no animal products at all, Sissy's vegetable stock is a hearty alternative.

4	tablespoons vegetable oil
2	large onions, peeled and sliced
2	carrots, sliced
2	garlic heads, halved
4	celery ribs, chopped
2	leeks, washed and sliced
4	sprigs thyme
4	sprigs tarragon
4	sprigs rosemary
4	whole allspice berries
4	bay leaves

Heat the oil in a large stockpot. Add the onion and cook until slightly wilted. Add the carrots, garlic, celery, leeks, thyme, tarragon, rosemary, allspice, bay leaves, and 6 quarts (24 cups) cold water. Bring to a simmer and cook for 1 hour uncovered. Strain through a fine-mesh strainer. Let cool, put into smaller containers, and refrigerate or freeze.

MAKES 6 QUARTS

Note: You can freeze the stock in small containers or ice cube trays, allowing you to use what you need at a later time.

Veal Stock

Veal stock is an essential ingredient in many of my sauces," Sissy notes. "Once you make a batch, it will keep for up to three days refrigerated and up to two months frozen." She suggests freezing the stock in plastic ice cube trays, so if you need only a small amount, you can pop out as many cubes as you need.

4	pounds veal knuckles	1	head garlic, halved
½	cup tomato paste	2	sprigs each of thyme, tarragon, sage, and rosemary
1	large onion, halved		
1	carrot, sliced	2	bay leaves
1	leek, sliced	1	tablespoon black peppercorns
2	celery ribs, sliced		

Preheat the oven to 425°F. Put the veal knuckles spread with the tomato paste in a deep roasting pan. Put the pan in the oven. After 30 minutes, add the onion, carrot, leek, celery, and garlic. Roast about 40 minutes more or until the bones are deeply browned. Remove from the oven. With a sturdy pair of tongs, transfer the bones and vegetables to a very large stockpot. Pour off and discard any excess fat from the roasting pan, and place the pan over medium heat. When the pan is hot, pour in 2 cups water. Scrape up any brown drippings from the bottom of the pan. Add this drippings mixture to the stockpot. Add the herbs and peppercorns and 6 quarts (24 cups) cold water. Slowly bring the stock to a simmer over medium heat. This will take about 45 minutes. Skim off any fat or foam that rises to the surface. Continue to simmer slowly, uncovered, for 6 hours, skimming as needed. Strain the stock through a fine mesh strainer and discard the solids. To cool, pour the stock into a large kettle in a sink filled with cold water. Stir the stock occasionally. If the water in the sink becomes too warm, drain and refill with cold water. When the stock is completely cool, pour into containers, cover, and refrigerate or freeze.

MAKES 6 QUARTS

Note: You can freeze the stock in small containers or ice cube trays, allowing you to use what you need at a later time.

Duck Stock

Useful in soups, rice, and risotto, duck stock can be made whenever you have leftover duck carcasses.

3	duck carcasses	3	sprigs thyme
2	onions, halved	3	sprigs rosemary
2	carrots, cut into 3 pieces	4	bay leaves
2	celery ribs, cut into 3 pieces		Peppercorns
1	garlic head, cut in half		

Preheat the oven to 450°F. In a deep roasting pan, roast the duck carcasses, turning after 15 minutes. The ducks will begin to brown after 30 minutes. Add the onions, carrots, celery, and garlic. Continue to roast for another 30 minutes. Remove from the oven. Using tongs, transfer the carcasses and vegetables to a large stockpot. Pour off and discard any excess fat from the roasting pan and place the pan over medium heat. When the pan is hot, pour in 2 cups water. Scrape up any brown drippings from the bottom of the pan. Add this drippings mixture to the stockpot. Add the thyme, rosemary, bay leaves, and peppercorns and 6 quarts (24 cups) cold water, enough to cover the bones. Over medium heat, slowly bring the stock to a simmer. This will take about 45 minutes. Skim off any fat or foam that rises to the surface. Continue to simmer the stock slowly, uncovered, for 3 hours, skimming as needed. Strain the stock through a fine mesh strainer and discard the solids. To cool, place the stock into a large kettle in a sink filled with cold water. Stir the stock occasionally. If the water in the sink becomes too warm, drain and refill with cold water. When the stock is completely cooled, pour it into containers and cover. It will keep refrigerated for up to two days, or frozen up to three months.

MAKES 6 QUARTS

Note: You can freeze the stock in small containers or ice cube trays, allowing you to use what you need at a later time.

Tomato-Cucumber Relish

Here is a bright-flavored relish that pairs well with seafood, especially when the tomatoes are garden fresh. Also, it's good as a salad all by itself—a harvest meal, when you have too many great tomatoes on hand.

4	fresh plum tomatoes, diced
2	cucumbers, peeled, seeded, and thinly sliced
6	sprigs dill, chopped
1	red onion, thinly sliced
½	cup olive oil
2	tablespoons lemon juice
	Salt and pepper

In a medium bowl toss together the tomatoes, cucumbers, dill, onion, olive oil, lemon juice, and salt and pepper to taste. Put in a container and refrigerate.

MAKES ABOUT 3 CUPS

Vegetable Dishes

&

Ratatouille

Eggplant Crêpes

Grilled Polenta with Oyster and Portobello Mushrooms

Mushroom Stroganoff

Veggie Burgers

Lentil Pilaf

Orange-Scented Black Beans

Purée of Celery Root with Apples

Curried Corn Pudding

Puréed Yams

Baked Spaghetti Squash

White Beans

Brown Basmati Rice

Braised Red Cabbage with Apples

Sauerkraut

Polenta

Baked Acorn Squash with
Root Vegetables and Black Beans

Moroccan Vegetable Stew

Ratatouille

When eggplants, zucchini, and fresh tomatoes are abundant, this is the perfect classic vegetarian casserole for the summer harvest. Sissy says she makes huge batches of ratatouille and freezes it to be used through the winter.

1	*pound eggplant, sliced in ½-inch rounds*
1	*pound zucchini, sliced in ½-inch rounds*
	Salt
1	*pound onions, sliced*
¼	*pound green peppers, seeded and sliced*
6	*plus 4 tablespoons olive oil*
2	*pounds fresh tomatoes, poached and peeled*
1	*tablespoon minced garlic*
1	*cup fresh basil leaves*
	Pepper

Toss the sliced eggplant and zucchini separately with salt to taste. Let stand for about 1 hour. Meanwhile, sauté the onions and peppers in 4 tablespoons oil. When soft, slightly crush the tomatoes with your hands and add to the sauté pan. Add the garlic and basil and cook for about 10 minutes. Remove from the heat. Add salt if needed and the pepper to taste.

Preheat the oven to 350°F. Rinse the zucchini and eggplant and pat dry with paper towels. In a large sauté pan, using the remaining 6 tablespoons oil, sauté the eggplant, then the zucchini separately until slightly soft. In a casserole dish, layer the eggplant and zucchini with the tomato mixture. Cover the casserole and bake for 30 minutes.

MAKES 8 TO 10 SERVINGS

Eggplant Crêpes

A perfect vegetarian meal" is how Sissy describes this dish in which the crêpe is the eggplant itself, stuffed with spinach and ricotta and baked.

2	medium to large eggplants
6	cups water
1	tablespoon butter
2	pounds spinach, washed
2	cups ricotta cheese
½	cup vegetable oil
	Salt
	Mozzarella cheese
	Tomato Sauce (see page 126)

Trim the tops, peel the eggplants, and stand them on end. With a sharp knife, slice them thinly lengthwise, approximately six slices per eggplant. Put the slices in a colander and generously salt between the layers. Let stand for approximately 1 hour. In the meantime, make the spinach stuffing. Put the water and 1 teaspoon salt in a medium pot. Bring to a boil. Submerge the spinach and let it cook for about 5 minutes. (You can steam the spinach instead.) Drain the spinach, cool, and squeeze dry. Put the spinach in a food processor and chop it coarsely. You don't want it to purée; I like some texture. Put the spinach in a mixing bowl and add the ricotta. Mix with a rubber spatula. Refrigerate until you are ready to roll the eggplant crêpes.

Preheat the oven to 400°F. Thoroughly rinse the salt from the eggplant and pat dry. Rub some of the oil on a flat sheet pan. Arrange the eggplant pieces on the sheet without overlapping. Roast for 7 minutes. Then flip the slices over and cook for another 7 minutes. Remove the eggplant slices from the oven and let cool. (I like to take the eggplant off the tray immediately, so the slices don't soak up all the oil.) After the eggplant has cooled, place the slices on the countertop. Fill and roll each eggplant slice lengthwise with the spinach and ricotta mixture. Put them into a container until ready to assemble.

To assemble the crêpes, spread some of the tomato sauce on the bottom of a casserole dish (use enough to serve with the crêpes). Put in the eggplant rolls, and top with a small amount of sauce and fresh mozzarella cheese, one piece per crêpe. Refrigerate until ready to use. When ready to bake, preheat the oven to 400°F and cook for about 45 minutes. The cheese will be nicely melted, and the sauce will be bubbly.

MAKES 12 CRÉPES

IN THE MARBLE VALLEY

When colonists settled in southern Vermont in 1768, they thought they saw vast snow banks along Dorset Mountain. The great white streaks turned out to be marble, and the abundance of it buried under the mountains that surround what became known as the "marble valley" made Dorset a thriving enterprise zone through much of the nineteenth century.

The United States' first quarry opened in Dorset in 1785. The rich lode under the mountains that surrounded the town first went to headstones, doorsills, and hearths in the region, but when the Bennington-Rutland rail line was completed in 1852 and transportation beyond the region improved, great hunks of it were shipped farther. Some went to the battlefields of Gettysburg, where five thousand of the headstones were made of Dorset marble. Some went on to to Washington for the U.S. Supreme Court building. And some went to Cambridge for the Harvard Medical School building. Throughout the Northeast, courthouses, churches, banks, and libraries were built from it. It is estimated that over fifteen million cubic feet of Dorset marble was mined from local quarries between 1785 and 1918. Much of it bears a telltale pattern of pale blue and green veins streaking through the smooth white rock.

Late in the 1890s, as the U.S. economy slumped, Dorset's marble business was hit especially hard because better and more colorful grades of stone were being harvested in Rutland and Proctor. Furthermore, Dorset marble had a reputation for being relatively soft. Italian marble, which became more readily available, was harder. Things looked up temporarily in 1900 when construction began on the New

York Public Library, much of which was made of Dorset marble. Completion of the library in 1911 was the death knell for local quarries, most of which were closed by the 1920s.

Today, the town's first quarry, which was later the one that sent stone to the New York Public Library as well as to the D.A.R. building in Washington, is a favorite summer swimming hole and picnic area. Trails lead from the side of Route 30 into a fabulous maze of great white stone blocks that surround pools with an emerald green tint caused by run-off from the marble. When no one is swimming, the water is still, reflecting trees, sky, and rock as clearly as a mirror.

Grilled Polenta with Oyster and Portobello Mushrooms

A great vegetarian dinner served with a large salad of arugula or spinach or with sautéed spinach.

2	tablespoons vegetable oil
1	medium white onion, sliced
1	teaspoon minced garlic
½	leek, julienned
1	tablespoon minced fresh sage
1	tablespoon minced fresh thyme
1	tablespoon minced fresh tarragon
1	tablespoon minced fresh rosemary
3	cups water
½	teaspoon salt
¼	teaspoon pepper
8	ounces yellow cornmeal
¼	pound garlic butter
¼	cup garlic oil*
½	pound shiitake mushrooms
½	pound oyster mushrooms
½	pound portobello mushrooms
3	cups Tomato Coulis (see page 127)
4	ounces shaved Asiago cheese

Heat the oil in a medium-size saucepan over medium heat. Add the onion, garlic, and leek and cook until softened. Add the sage, thyme, tarragon, and rosemary, the water, salt, and pepper. Bring to a boil and reduce the heat to a simmer. Start adding the cornmeal, sifting it through your hand while you whisk constantly with the other hand. The polenta mixture will become fairly thick. At that point, use a wooden spoon to stir. Stir for about 5 more minutes and taste for seasoning. Turn into a loaf pan to chill. When chilled, cut into squares to grill or sauté in a little butter until browned on both sides. Keep warm in a low oven (200°F) while you sauté the mushrooms.

Heat the garlic butter and garlic oil in a large sauté pan. When the butter is slightly melted, add the mushrooms and sauté on low heat until the mushrooms are soft. Remove from the heat.

To serve: Spoon the Tomato Coulis on six plates. Place the grilled or sautéed polenta on top. Divide the mushrooms among the plates and top with the Asiago cheese.

MAKES 6 SERVINGS

*Note: For the garlic oil, in a medium saucepan heat 2 cups olive or vegetable oil and 12 peeled and crushed garlic cloves on low heat for about 1 hour. Be sure to keep the heat low so the garlic doesn't burn. Store in the refrigerator.

Mushroom Stroganoff

I have many vegetarian guests, so I'm always trying new interesting dishes," Sissy says. "When my friend, Ed Sargent, goes foraging for mushrooms, he always stops at the inn." I believe that stroganoff brings out the taste of the mushrooms."

2	tablespoons Garlic Oil (see note on page 155)
1	cup thinly sliced onion
½	pound shiitake mushrooms, stemmed but not sliced
½	pound cremini mushrooms, stemmed and quartered
½	pound portobello mushrooms, stemmed and sliced
½	pound oyster mushrooms, whole
1	tablespoon fresh tarragon or 1 teaspoon dried
1	tablespoon fresh sage or 1 teaspoon dried
1	teaspoon salt
1	teaspoon pepper
½	cup sun-dried tomatoes, rehydrated and julienned
1	tablespoon tomato paste
1	tablespoon Worcestershire sauce
1	cup mushroom stock
2	cups sour cream
	Pappardelle for serving

Heat the garlic oil in a saucepan over medium-high heat. Add the onions and cook until slightly wilted. Add the mushrooms, tarragon, sage, salt, and pepper and sauté until soft. Add the tomatoes, tomato paste, Worcestershire sauce, and stock. Bring to a simmer and reduce about 5 minutes. Using a rubber spatula, gently stir in the sour cream. Cook until the mixture is heated through. Serve over pappardelle (or other type of noodle or rice).

MAKES 6 SERVINGS

Variation: Use morel or chanterelle mushrooms if they are in season.

 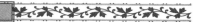

Veggie Burgers

Sissy notes, "With the spa in house, I want to offer light cuisine and healthy alternatives. That is why I came up with these veggie burgers, which are hugely popular, and not only among strict vegetarians."

½	cup bulgur wheat		2	garlic cloves
1	cup boiling water		2	tablespoons vegetable oil
1	medium carrot, peeled and cut into ¾-inch pieces		1	teaspoon salt
			½	teaspoon pepper
1	parsnip, peeled and cut into ¾-inch pieces		1	teaspoon cumin
			½	teaspoon curry powder
1	red pepper, seeded and halved		½	cup cooked, chopped spinach
1	yellow pepper, seeded and halved		1	(15-ounce) can garbanzo beans
1	medium onion, quartered			
1	cup broccoli florets			

Preheat the oven to 350°F. In a small bowl soak the bulgur in the boiling water for 20 minutes. In a large mixing bowl toss the carrot, parsnip, peppers, onion, broccoli, and garlic with the oil, salt, pepper, cumin, and curry powder. Spread the vegetables on a rimmed baking sheet and roast for 15 minutes or until tender. In the work bowl of a food processor, combine the roasted vegetables, spinach, and garbanzo beans. Pulse until the mixture is well combined. Transfer to a mixing bowl, mix together with the bulgar, and form into patties. Place the patties onto a well greased baking sheet and bake for about 8 minutes or until heated through. Serve with the Roasted Red Pepper Sauce (see page 139) and sautéed spinach..

MAKES 6 SERVINGS

Lentil Pilaf

Bulgur and lentils combine to make an immensely satisfying meal. We don't mind dolloping on some of the harissa (see page 170) that is used on the Moroccan Vegetable Stew.

2	tablespoons vegetable oil
½	medium onion, diced
½	carrot, diced
½	celery rib, diced
2	tablespoons minced garlic
1½	tablespoons minced fresh ginger
1	cup brown lentils
1	tablespoon miso
½	teaspoon salt
¼	teaspoon ground black pepper
3	cups water or stock
1	cup bulgur wheat

Heat the oil in a medium saucepan. Add the onion, carrot, celery, garlic, and ginger. Sauté until the vegetables are soft, about 5 minutes. Add the lentils and miso and stir. Add the salt, pepper, and water or stock. Bring to a boil and reduce to medium heat. Let the mixture simmer, uncovered, about 20 minutes or until the lentils are soft. Add the bulgur and let simmer about 5 minutes more. Turn off the heat, put a lid on the saucepan and let stand about 10 minutes or until the bulgur is soft. Fluff with a fork.

MAKES 4 TO 6 SERVINGS

Orange-Scented Black Beans

A smoky hint of poblano peppers and the sting of jalapeño make black beans dance with alluring flavor.

1	teaspoon olive oil
1	medium onion, peeled and chopped
3	to 4 garlic cloves, crushed
1	small jalapeño, seeded and minced
1	cup black beans, soaked in water for 8 to 10 hours and drained
3	cups water
1½	teaspoons grated orange zest
1	teaspoon salt
	Black pepper
4	poblano peppers, roasted, peeled, seeded and cut into ½-inch dice
3	tablespoons thinly sliced scallions
	White rice for serving

Heat the oil in a large saucepan over medium heat. Add the onion and cook for 5 minutes. Reduce the heat to low. Add the garlic and jalapeño and cook, stirring frequently, for 2 minutes. Add the beans and water. Increase the heat and bring to a boil. Lower the heat so the liquid simmers and cook for 1¼ hours. Stir in the orange zest and continue cooking until the beans are tender, about 20 minutes longer. Season with the salt and add pepper to taste. Stir in the roasted peppers. Top with sliced scallions and serve with white rice.

MAKES 4 TO 5 SERVINGS

Purée of Celery Root with Apples

Sissy suggests that the rich flavor of celery root purée goes especially well with Duck Confit (see page 81) or a roast loin of pork.

2	pounds celery root, peeled and cut into 1-inch chunks
1	teaspoon salt
2	McIntosh apples, peeled and cut into 1-inch chunks
¼	cup heavy cream

Put the celery root in a medium saucepan and cover with water. Add the salt and bring to a boil. Reduce the heat and simmer for about 20 minutes. Add the apples and simmer another 5 minutes. Drain in a colander. Purée the mixture in a food processor while slowly adding the cream. Taste for seasoning.

MAKES 6 SERVINGS

Curried Corn Pudding

Excellent as a side vegetable with baked ham or roast pork.

1	tablespoon butter
½	cup minced onion
½	cup minced green pepper
1	tablespoon curry powder
2	cups cooked corn
3	eggs

2   cups heavy cream
1   teaspoon salt
½   teaspoon sugar

Preheat the oven to 350°F. Heat the butter in a medium-size saucepan over medium heat. Sauté the onion and green pepper. Stir in the curry powder and the corn. Mix together the eggs, heavy cream, salt, and sugar in a mixing bowl. Add the onion-corn mixture. Spoon the mixture into a buttered casserole dish and bake, uncovered, for 45 minutes.

MAKES 4 TO 6 SERVINGS

Puréed Yams

Although yams and sweet potatoes can be used interchangeably in recipes, they are in fact from two different species of plant. Yams tend to be sweeter and more moist.

3   yams or sweet potatoes, peeled and cut into chunks
4   tablespoons (½ stick) butter
1   teaspoon ground nutmeg
½   teaspoon ground cinnamon
½   teaspoon salt
½   teaspoon black pepper
¼   cup maple syrup

Preheat the oven to 350°F. Put the yams into a roasting pan. Cut the butter into small chunks and mix with the yams. Sprinkle with the nutmeg, cinnamon, salt, and pepper, and pour the syrup on top. Cover with aluminum foil and bake for 15 to 20 minutes or until the yams are just soft. Put the yams in a food processor and purée.

MAKES 4 TO 6 SERVINGS

Baked Spaghetti Squash

Also known as vegetable spaghetti, spaghetti squash does an amazing transformation act when it is cooked. The flesh transforms into long strands that resemble spaghetti noodles.

1	to 2 medium spaghetti squash, halved and seeded
4	tablespoons garlic butter (see page 42)
	Salt and pepper

Preheat the oven to 350°F. Place the squash cut side up in a large roasting pan. Put the garlic butter in the center with the salt and pepper to taste. Cover the pan with aluminum foil and bake for about 45 minutes. Don't overcook the squash because it will wilt into mush. When done, scrape the squash out of the shell with a fork. You can serve as spaghetti with pesto or tomato sauce and topped with grated Asiago cheese. What great texture!

MAKES 4 TO 6 SERVINGS

White Beans

Sissy's suggested use for white beans is to serve them under lamb shanks (see page 102).

1	tablespoon vegetable oil
2	shallots, minced
2	garlic cloves, minced
1	carrot, diced
1	celery rib, diced
½	leek, diced
1	sprig rosemary
1	sprig thyme
1	pound dried navy or Great Northern beans, soaked for 3 hours
	Salt and pepper
6	cups chicken stock or water
1	cup canned whole tomatoes

Heat the oil in a large saucepan over medium heat. Add the shallots, garlic, carrot, celery, leek, rosemary, and thyme. Cook until softened, approximately 5 minutes. Drain and rinse the beans and add them to the pan. Stir and add the salt and pepper. Add the chicken stock. Cover and let simmer until the beans are tender, approximately 1 hour. Just before they are finished add the canned tomatoes and stir.

MAKES 6 SERVINGS

Brown Basmati Rice

Basmati rice has a fetching, perfumy aroma and nut-rich flavor that make it a serious side dish or underpinning for a vegetable medley.

2	*tablespoons vegetable oil*
½	*medium white onion, minced*
2	*teaspoons minced fresh ginger*
2	*teaspoons minced garlic*
¼	*cup diced celery*
¼	*cup diced carrot*
¼	*cup diced leek*
1	*cup basmati rice*
1½	*cups vegetable stock (or water)*

Heat the oil in a medium-size saucepan over medium hear. Add the onion, ginger, garlic, celery, carrot, and leek. Cook until the onion is soft, about 5 minutes. Add the rice and stir until blended with the vegetables. Add the stock or water and bring to a boil. Reduce the heat, cover, and simmer until all the liquid is absorbed and the rice is soft, about 15 minutes.

MAKES 4 TO 6 SERVINGS

Braised Red Cabbage with Apples

Braised red cabbage is a necessary side dish for the Duck Confit (see page 81). It is tangy and sweet, and it brings out the rich flavors of the meat.

2	to 2 ½ pounds red cabbage, shredded
⅔	cup red wine vinegar
2	tablespoons sugar
2	teaspoons salt
2	tablespoons bacon fat (or vegetable oil)
2	apples, peeled and diced
½	cup finely chopped onions
1	whole onion, pierced with 2 cloves
1	small bay leaf
1	cup boiling water
3	tablespoons dry red wine

Combine the red cabbage, red wine vinegar, sugar, and salt in a large mixing bowl. Let marinate overnight, or at least a couple of hours. Heat the bacon fat or oil in a medium-size stainless steel pot over medium heat. When hot, carefully add the red cabbage mixture. Add the apples, chopped onions, whole onion, and bay leaf and cook until slightly wilted. Add the water and red wine. Cover and cook at a slow simmer for about 1 hour, stirring occasionally. The cabbage will darken and soften as it cooks. Add more wine as necessary. Remove the clove-studded onion before serving.

MAKES 4 TO 6 SERVINGS

Note: This will hold for up to a week in the refrigerator. The longer it sits the better it tastes.

Sauerkraut

Sissy makes a wonderful Ruben sandwich with this sauerkraut. It holds up great in the refrigerator for a week. It's also good with different sausages, such as knockwurst, bockwurst, or bratwurst.

2	tablespoons vegetable oil
4	strips bacon, diced
2	(1-pound) bags sauerkraut, drained
1	onion, minced
2	juniper berries
2	sprigs thyme, minced (or 1 teaspoon dried)
2	sprigs sage, minced (or 1 teaspoon dried)
1	potato, diced
	Salt and pepper
1	plus ¼ bottles inexpensive, dry white wine
6	cups chicken stock (see page 141)

Heat the oil in a medium-size saucepan over medium heat. Add the bacon and cook until wilted, not crisp. You want to render most of the fat. Remove the bacon. Turn the heat to high and very carefully add the sauerkraut. Brown the sauerkraut quickly in the bacon fat. Reduce the heat to medium. Toss and stir for about 10 minutes. It should be nicely browned. Add the onion, juniper berries, thyme, sage, potato, and salt and pepper to taste. Pour in 1 bottle white wine. Let the mixture cook down for about 15 minutes and then add the remaining ¼ bottle wine as needed. Cook for another 15 minutes. The wine should be almost cooked out of the sauerkraut. Finish off with the chicken stock, and let the mixture cook down until there is little liquid remaining.

MAKES 6 TO 8 SERVINGS

Polenta

Polenta is usually a side dish, but it also can be a main meal when topped with freshly stewed tomatoes and Asiago cheese.

4	tablespoons (½ stick) butter
½	leek, sliced
1	teaspoon minced garlic
4	cups water or vegetable stock
½	teaspoon salt
1	cup cornmeal
½	cup rehydrated sun-dried tomatoes, julienned
½	cup basil, julienned
¼	cup cream cheese

Melt the butter in a medium-size saucepan over medium heat, add the leek and garlic, and cook for about 3 minutes. Add the water or stock and salt and bring to a boil. Turn down to a simmer, and slowly add the cornmeal, sifting it through one hand and whisking with the other. Keep whisking until all the cornmeal is used up. When it begins to thicken stir with a wooden spoon for about 10 minutes. Remove from the heat and stir in the sun-dried tomatoes, basil, and cream cheese. The polenta will stiffen after it sits for a bit. Keep stirring until it is a nice soft consistency.

MAKES 6 TO 8 SERVINGS

Baked Acorn Squash with Root Vegetables and Black Beans

A hearty vegetarian meal that is an especially good winter dish.

Black Beans

2	teaspoons olive oil
1	small onion, peeled and diced
2	teaspoons minced garlic
1	pound dried black beans, rinsed and soaked for 6 to 8 hours
6	cups water or vegetable broth

Acorn Squash

3	acorn squash, split in half lengthwise
6	tablespoons butter
	Salt and pepper

Curried Vegetables

2	tablespoons vegetable oil
1	small onion, chopped
3	garlic cloves, minced
1	2-inch piece fresh ginger, peeled and minced
1½	teaspoons curry powder
4	cups vegetable broth
2	medium carrots, peeled, halved lengthwise, cut into ½-inch slices
2	large parsnips, peeled, halved lengthwise, cut into ⅛-inch slices
1	small celery root, trimmed, peeled, and cut into ¼-inch cubes
2	turnips, peeled, halved lengthwise, cut into ½-inch lengths
1	medium sweet potato, peeled and cut into 1-inch cubes
3	tablespoons butter

3   tablespoons all-purpose flour

2   teaspoons salt

      Freshly ground pepper

1   tablespoon chopped Italian parsley

Assembly

      Curried Vegetables

1½   cups black beans

1   cup sour cream

1   cup sliced scallions

In a large saucepan over medium heat, add the oil and sauté the onion and the garlic until soft. Add the black beans. Cover with the water or broth, bring to a boil, and simmer, covered, for 1½ to 2 hours until the beans are soft. Drain all but ½ cup of the liquid.

Make the acorn squash. Preheat the oven to 350°F. Put 1 tablespoon butter in each squash half and season with salt and pepper to taste. Place the squash in a roasting pan and add enough water to cover the bottom of the pan. Cover the pan with foil and bake for 40 to 50 minutes until the squash is fork tender.

While the squash are cooking, prepare the curried vegetables. Heat the oil in a large pot over medium heat. Add the onion, garlic, and ginger and cook for 3 minutes. Stir in the curry powder and cook for 30 seconds. Add the broth, carrots, and parsnips. Bring to a simmer, reduce the heat, cover, and cook for 15 minutes. Stir in the celery root, turnips, and sweet potato and cook 10 minutes longer. Remove from the heat. In a small saucepan over medium heat, melt the butter. Add the flour. Stir and lightly brown the mixture for a minute or so, and then add 1 cup of the liquid in which the vegetables were simmered. Cook until thickened and add back to the vegetables. Add the salt, pepper to taste, and the parsley.

To assemble spoon equal amounts of the black beans and then equal amounts of the curried vegetables into each squash half, top with a dollop of sour cream, and sprinkle with the chopped scallions.

MAKES 6 SERVINGS

Moroccan Vegetable Stew

Serve Moroccan vegetable stew with Israeli couscous and harissa. The couscous can be made ahead and heated up by steaming it in a cheesecloth-lined colander over some broth from the stew.

4	plus 4 tablespoons vegetable oil
1	plus 1 large onions, peeled and sliced
1	tablespoon minced fresh ginger
⅛	teaspoon saffron, about 3 threads
¼	teaspoon ground cinnamon
¼	teaspoon turmeric
¼	teaspoon ground nutmeg
½	cup minced parsley
¼	cup cilantro leaves
3½	cups vegetable stock (see page 142)
1	teaspoon salt
1	teaspoon pepper
2	carrots, peeled and cut into 3-inch lengthwise pieces
2	small zucchini, cut into 3-inch lengthwise pieces
2	small yellow squash, cut into 3-inch lengthwise pieces
¼	cup honey
½	cup raisins
2	tomatoes, diced
	Slivered almonds, chickpeas, and cilantro for garnish

Harissa

2	garlic cloves
2	jalapeño peppers, seeded and chopped
1	teaspoon crushed red pepper flakes
4	teaspoons caraway seeds

1	teaspoon ground cumin
1	teaspoon ground coriander
1	teaspoon salt
½	teaspoon black pepper
1	tablespoon olive oil

Couscous

1	tablespoon vegetable oil
1	shallot, finely minced
2	garlic cloves, finely minced
1	tomato, diced
3	cups vegetable stock
2	cups Israeli couscous
	Salt and pepper

Heat 4 tablespoons oil in a medium-size pot over medium heat. Sauté 1 onion with the ginger. Add the saffron, cinnamon, turmeric, nutmeg, parsley, and cilantro. Stir. Add the vegetable stock, salt, and pepper. Bring to a simmer and drop in the carrots. Simmer until the carrots just begin to soften, about 6 minutes; then add the zucchini and yellow squash. Simmer another 5 minutes. Heat the remaining 4 tablespoons oil in another sauté pan over medium heat. Add the remaining onion, the honey, raisins, and tomatoes. Sauté until the onions are soft and then add this mixture to the vegetable mixture. Simmer for another 5 minutes. The vegetables will be soft but not mushy. Garnish with the slivered almonds, chickpeas, and cilantro leaves.

Prepare the Harissa. Place the garlic, jalapeño peppers, pepper flakes, caraway seeds, cumin, coriander, salt, pepper, and olive oil in the bowl of a food processor and purée. Put in a container and refrigerate.

For the couscous, heat the oil in a medium saucepan over medium heat. Sauté the shallot, garlic, and tomato until just soft. Add the vegetable stock and bring to a simmer. Add the couscous and salt and pepper to taste and stir. Bring back to a simmer, remove from the heat, and cover. Let sit for about 15 minutes. Once the couscous has absorbed all the liquid, serve with the stew along with the Harissa.

MAKES 12 SERVINGS

Pasta
&

Angel Hair Pasta with
Chanterelle Mushrooms and Gorgonzola Cheese

Chicken Cannelloni

Linguini with Bolognese Sauce

Parpadelle with Vegetable Bolognese

Pasta with Duck, Mushrooms, and Spinach

Chilled Curried Mussels and Fettuccine

Penne with Grilled Vegetables and
Black Olive Sun-Dried Tomato Pesto

Angel Hair Pasta with Chanterelle Mushrooms and Gorgonzola Cheese

Sissy explains that she developed this dish during chanterelle mushroom season when she found herself with plenty of ripe pears and local Gorgonzola cheese. "I wanted to incorporate them all into a really light dish," she says. "I like this because you can really taste the flavor of the mushrooms."

4	tablespoons olive oil
3	shallots, julienned
3	ripe Bosc pears, sliced
1	leek, julienned
1	sprig fresh sage, minced
¼	pound fresh (or dry, rehydrated) chanterelle mushrooms
	Salt and pepper
1	cup white wine
1	pound angel hair pasta, cooked
1	cup Gorgonzola cheese, crumbled

Heat the oil in a medium-size sauté pan. Add the shallots and caramelize them over a medium flame. Add the pears, leek, minced sage, mushrooms, and salt and pepper to taste. Cook until the pears and mushrooms are just barely soft. Add the wine and reduce for about 5 minutes. Add the pasta to the pan and mix well. Toss with the Gorgonzola cheese.

MAKES 6 SERVINGS

Chicken Cannelloni

Sissy dedicates this recipe to her good friend Arthur Silverman, a local who orders it every time he comes to eat.

2	tablespoons vegetable oil
½	onion, diced
1	tablespoon minced garlic
2	cups chicken tenderloins
1	tablespoon mixed fresh herbs (rosemary, thyme, tarragon and sage)
½	cup sliced shiitake mushrooms
¼	pound spinach
	Salt and pepper
2	cups ricotta cheese
3	sheets fresh pasta or 12 cannelloni shells, cooked according to package directions
3	cups Tomato Sauce (see page 126)

Béchamel Sauce

1	cup milk
1	cup half-and-half
4	tablespoons roux
½	teaspoon salt
	Black pepper

Grated Parmesan or Asiago cheese

Preheat the oven to 350°F. In a medium-size sauté pan heat the oil over a medium flame, and sauté the onion and garlic until wilted. Lower the heat and add the chicken meat. Cook the chicken through, and add the herbs, mushrooms, and spinach. Cook until the mushrooms are soft and the spinach is wilted. Add the salt and pepper to taste. Drain the mixture in a colander and cool. Place the mixture in a food processor and pulse briefly until coarsely ground. Remove to a bowl and mix in the ricotta cheese. If using fresh pasta sheets, quarter them into 4 x 4-inch pieces. Place equal amounts of the filling on each piece. Turn the pasta over the filling to form rolls. Coat the bottom of a large baking dish with fresh Tomato Sauce. Put in the cannelloni and cover with the rest of the tomato sauce.

Prepare the Béchamel Sauce. In a small saucepan scald the milk and half-and-half on low heat. Simmer while whisking in the roux, salt, and pepper to taste. Whisk until thickened and coats the back of a spoon. Pour the béchamel over all. Sprinkle with Parmesan. Place in the oven for 30 minutes until the sauce bubbles and the top is lightly browned.

MAKES 6 SERVINGS

Linguini with Bolognese Sauce

Named after the city of Bologna, which is known for its hearty cooking, Bolognese sauce is known to Italians as *ragù*. Sissy makes it from the scraps and trimmings off pork, veal and sirloin steak.

2	tablespoons olive oil
1	large onion, diced
1	green bell pepper, minced
2	tablespoons minced garlic (6 cloves)
2	carrots, diced
4	celery ribs, diced
½	pound ground veal (optional)
½	pound ground pork (optional)
½	pound ground beef, or use all beef in place of veal and pork
1	teaspoon dried red pepper flakes (optional)
2	teaspoons dried oregano
2	teaspoons dried basil
2	(28-ounce) cans crushed tomatoes
	Salt and pepper
	Grated Parmesan or Asiago cheese
1½	pounds linguini

Heat the oil in a large sauté pan or a pot over medium heat. Add the onion, pepper, garlic, carrots, and celery. Cook until wilted, but not browned, and add the meat. Toss and stir until the meat is fully browned and cooked. Add the red pepper flakes, oregano, basil, and tomatoes. Add salt and pepper to taste. Let simmer for about 30 minutes. Top with the grated Parmesan.

While the sauce is simmering, boil the linguini for 10 minutes or until al dente. Serve the linguini with Bolognese over the top.

MAKES ABOUT 8 CUPS

Parpadelle with Vegetable Bolognese

A rainbow of vegetables gives this meatless meal a festive flavor. Sissy suggests that instead of pasta, it can also top soft polenta or be used as a layer in lasagna.

1	pound parpadelle
2	tablespoons olive oil
1	large onion, sliced
2	green bell peppers, seeded and diced
2	tablespoons minced garlic
1	eggplant, not peeled, ½-inch dice, salted for about 1 hour, rinsed well and dried
2	small zucchini, diced
2	small yellow squash, diced
2	carrots, diced
	Salt and pepper
2	teaspoons dried oregano
2	teaspoons dried basil
2	(28-ounce) cans crushed tomatoes

Cook the pasta according to package directions; drain. Heat the oil in a medium saucepan over medium heat. Add the onion, pepper, and garlic and cook until soft. Add the eggplant, zucchini, yellow squash, carrots, salt and pepper, dried oregano, and basil. Cook until soft, stirring occasionally. Add the tomatoes and let simmer for about 30 minutes. Toss with the pasta and serve.

MAKES 6 SERVINGS

Pasta with Duck, Mushrooms, and Spinach

When I cut up ducks for confit, I pull the little tenderloins off and freeze them until I have accumulated enough," Sissy says. "Then I make pasta with duck, mushrooms, and spinach."

2	pounds pasta (linguine, penne, or fusille)
4	tablespoons rosemary oil
2	shallots, sliced
48	duck tenders, approximately 8 per person
1	sprig rosemary, minced
1	sprig sage, minced
1	sprig tarragon, minced
2	sprigs thyme, minced
12	shiitake mushrooms, sliced
1	pound spinach, julienned
	Grated Parmesan or Asiago cheese
	Pepper

Cook the pasta according to package directions. Heat the oil in a large sauté pan over medium heat. Add the shallots and sauté until soft. Add the duck tenders. Add the rosemary, sage, tarragon, thyme, and the mushrooms. Sauté until the mushrooms are soft and the duck tenders are cooked through. Add the spinach and toss quickly. When the pasta is done cooking, transfer it to a large bowl and add the cooked duck mixture. Toss so the pasta is evenly coated with the oil. Sprinkle with grated Parmesan or Asiago cheese and freshly ground pepper to taste.

MAKES 6 SERVINGS

Chilled Curried Mussels and Fettuccine

Mussels are good hot or cold. Here they are the basis of a bright seafood mix with broad fettuccine noodles.

2	pounds fresh mussels
4	cups white wine
1	leek, julienned
1	tablespoon curry powder
2	teaspoons minced garlic
2	tablespoons butter
1	to 2 cups mayonnaise
2	pounds fettucine, cooked
	Minced parsley

Combine the mussels with the white wine, leeks, curry powder, minced garlic, and butter in a large sauté pan over medium-high heat. Cover, bring to a boil, and steam the mussels for about 5 minutes. All the mussels should open; throw away any that do not. Remove the mussels from the pan and strain the broth into a smaller saucepan. Simmer the broth and reduce by about half, approximately 15 minutes. Let cool. Add the reduced broth to the mayonnaise. (You will need 1 cup of mayonnaise for every 2 tablespoons of reduced broth.) Taste for seasoning. Remove the cooked mussels from the shells. Toss the mayonnaise mixture with the cooked fettuccine. Add the mussels and some minced parsley.

MAKES 8 SERVINGS

Penne with Grilled Vegetables and Black Olive Sun-Dried Tomato Pesto

At the end of the summer, when the harvest yields a bounty of vegetables, this is a great vegetarian dish.

2	medium zucchini	**Black Olive Sun-Dried Tomato Pesto**	
2	medium summer squash	1	cup pine nuts
1	eggplant	1	cup sun-dried tomatoes, rehydrated
1	red bell pepper	2	cups pitted kalamata olives
1	yellow bell pepper	1 ¼	cups crumbled feta cheese
½	cup julienne fresh basil	5	cups fresh basil, washed
2	teaspoons minced garlic	2	cups olive oil
1	cup olive or vegetable oil		
		2	pounds penne pasta cooked
			Grated Asiago cheese

Slice the zucchini and summer squash on a bias ¼-inch thick. Slice the eggplant, unpeeled, about ½-inch thick. Put in a colander, sprinkle with salt, and let sit for about 1 hour. Rinse and pat dry. Cut the peppers in half lengthwise and remove the seeds. In a large mixing bowl mix together the basil, garlic, and oil. Add the vegetables and marinate 2 hours at room temperature. Prepare a charcoal or gas grill. Bring to medium heat.

While heating the grill, prepare the pesto. In a food processor combine the pine nuts, sun-dried tomatoes, olives, cheese, and basil and pulse until roughly ground. While the processor is running, add the oil until blended.

Grill the vegetables, cooking until just soft. Cool and julienne the vegetables. Toss the vegetables with the pasta and add the pesto. Sprinkle with the Asiago cheese.

MAKES 6 SERVINGS

Dessert

Lemon Buttermilk Cake with Lemon Curd Sauce

Chocolate Mousse Cake

Rhubarb-Strawberry Crisp

Chocolate Terrine with Raspberry Sauce

Wild Rice Pudding

Crème Brûlée

White Chocolate Cheesecake

Lemon Squares

Rum Balls

Cider Sorbet with Red Wine Sauce

Peach and Blueberry Cobbler

Bread Pudding

My Mother's Pie Dough

White Chocolate Brownies

Blueberry Pie

Streusel Cream Peach Pie

Coconut Cream Pie

Banana Cream Pie

Lemon Buttermilk Cake with Lemon Curd Sauce

A sunshiny dessert that is sweet, moist, and oozing flavor.

Cake		**Lemon Curd Sauce**	
16	tablespoons (2 sticks) butter		Juice and grated zest of 6 lemons
2	plus ⅓ cups sugar	6	eggs
3	eggs	2	cups sugar
3	cups flour	12	tablespoons (1½ sticks) butter, softened
½	teaspoon baking soda		
½	teaspoon salt		
1	cup buttermilk		
	Zest of 2 to 3 lemons, grated		
½	cup plus 3 tablespoons lemon juice		
	Breadcrumbs or flour		

Preheat the oven to 350°F. Cream the butter with an electric mixer and add 2 cups sugar. Beat in the eggs one at a time. Sift together the flour, baking soda, and salt. Alternating (starting and ending with dry ingredients), add the dry ingredients and buttermilk to the mixture. Fold in the zest and 3 tablespoons lemon juice. Grease a Bundt pan, coat with the breadcrumbs or flour, and pour in the batter. Bake for 1 hour 15 minutes. Let the cake rest in the pan for 30 minutes.

While the cake is baking, make the lemon curd sauce. Combine the lemon juice and zest, eggs, and sugar in the top of a double boiler. Whisk over low heat until the mixture coats a spoon. Remove from the heat and whisk in the butter a small amount at a time. Refrigerate the sauce until ready to use.

Combine the remaining ⅓ cup sugar and the remaining ½ cup lemon juice in a saucepan. Heat until the sugar dissolves. Poke holes in the warm cake and pour the lemon juice mixture over the top. Let the syrup soak in for at least 15 minutes before turning out onto a tray or plate. Serve the cake with lemon curd sauce.

MAKES 12 SERVINGS

Chocolate Mousse Cake

Sissy developed chocolate mousse cake for her long-time friend and supporter, Joe Allen. "It's fairly simple to make," she says. "And it will hold in the refrigerator for a couple of days or can be frozen."

1	package Nabisco Famous Chocolate Wafers
½	cup confectioners' sugar
8	tablespoons (1 stick) butter, melted
10	ounces semi-sweet chocolate
⅓	cup hot water
2	egg yolks
1 ½	tablespoons granulated sugar
3	tablespoons Myer's rum
3	cups heavy cream (at room temperature)

Chop the chocolate wafers in a food processor with the confectioners' sugar. Put the mixture into a bowl and add the melted butter. Blend well and press into the sides and bottom of a springform pan. Put in the freezer. Heat the chocolate in the top of a small double boiler with the hot water. Heat until the chocolate is melted. Whisk the egg yolks and sugar over low heat until they are the consistency of pudding. Remove from the heat and whisk in the chocolate mixture and the rum. Cool. Whip the heavy cream until stiff. Fold into the chocolate mixture. It will be a mousse-like consistency. Pour into the crust and refrigerate or freeze 6 to 8 hours or overnight.

MAKES 8 TO 12 SERVINGS

Rhubarb-Strawberry Crisp

Yankee cookery is abundant with crisps, grunts, slumps, and cobblers, all of which are ways to combine fruit and sugar and crust. Rhubarb-Strawberry Crisp needn't be made with fresh berries, but if you do have good ones on hand, so much the better.

3	pounds rhubarb, cut into ½-inch pieces
1½	pints strawberries, cored
1	cup granulated sugar
1	plus ⅓ cups all-purpose flour
½	teaspoon ground cinnamon
8	tablespoons (1 stick) butter, cut into small pieces
1	cup light brown sugar
½	cup rolled oats
¾	cup chopped pecans

Preheat the oven to 375°F. Grease a 3-quart, rectangular baking dish. Combine the rhubarb, strawberries, sugar, ⅓ cup flour, and the cinnamon. Mix well and spread in the baking dish. For the topping combine the butter, the remaining 1 cup flour, brown sugar, oats, and pecans. Sprinkle the topping over the rhubarb and strawberry mixture. Bake for 35 to 45 minutes.

MAKES 12 SERVINGS

Chocolate Terrine with Raspberry Sauce

This recipe Sissy credits to Steve Johnson, a wonderful friend and chef who used to work at the Dorset Inn.

Chocolate Terrine

12	tablespoons (1½ sticks) unsalted butter
13	ounces semi-sweet chocolate chips
10	egg yolks
4	plus 1 tablespoons sugar
¾	cup heavy cream, whipped
2	egg whites, whipped to stiff peaks with a pinch of salt

Ganache

1	cup heavy cream
10	ounces semi-sweet chocolate chips

Raspberry Sauce

3	cups raspberries
½	cup sugar
½	cup water

Melt the butter and chocolate chips in the top of a double boiler over medium heat. Beat the egg yolks with 4 tablespoons sugar until thick and very pale in color. Fold the remaining tablespoon sugar into the egg yolk mixture and fold the egg mixture into the chocolate (still over the double boiler). Cook, stirring, until the mixture pulls away from the sides of the pan, about 8 minutes. Remove from the heat and fold in the heavy cream and egg whites. Pour the mixture into a one-pound loaf pan lined with plastic wrap and freeze 6 to 8 hours or overnight.

Before serving, prepare the ganache. Bring the cream to a boil in a heavy pan over medium-high heat and stir in the chocolate chips. Keep stirring until the chocolate is completely melted. Cool slightly and glaze the terrine with the mixture.

For the raspberry sauce, bring the raspberries, sugar, and water to a boil in a heavy pot over medium-high heat, stirring occasionally. Strain and cool. Refrigerate leftovers.

To remove from the mold, simply pull on the plastic wrap and the terrine should pop right out of the pan. Place on a serving dish and glaze with Ganache. To serve, slice the glazed terrine and pour some of the Raspberry Sauce over the top. Refrigerate leftovers.

MAKES 8 TO 10 SERVINGS

Wild Rice Pudding

"My friend Joe Allen's daughter Julie developed this recipe and was willing to share it with me," Sissy says. "It has the richness of crème brûlée, is very easy to assemble, and can be made a few days in advance."

1	*cup currants, soaked in brandy*
2	*cups cooked wild rice*
6	*cups heavy cream*
12	*egg yolks*
⅔	*cup sugar*
¼	*cup honey*
1	*teaspoon vanilla extract*

Preheat the oven to 275°F. Combine the currants and rice in a baking dish. Whisk the cream in a bowl with the egg yolks, sugar, honey, and vanilla. Pour over the rice mixture and place in a water bath. Bake for 1½ hours.

MAKES 12 SERVINGS

Crème Brûlée

What person with a sweet tooth doesn't love crème brûlée? It is smooth and rich and is actually quite easy to make. The only trick is the part at the end when you put the ramekins under the broiler. Watch them closely and constantly. You want the crust on top singed and teetering towards burnt, but not charred!

4	cups heavy cream
1	vanilla bean or 1 teaspoon vanilla extract
	Pinch of salt
9	egg yolks
¾	cup plus 2 tablespoons granulated sugar
9	tablespoons natural sugar or brown sugar

Combine the cream, vanilla, and salt in a saucepan and cook over medium heat for 5 minutes or until the mixture begins to "shimmer." Mix together the egg yolks and ¾ cup plus 2 tablespoons granulated sugar in a bowl. Add the cream mixture and stir until dissolved. Strain into another bowl and skim the air bubbles off the top. Pour into ten individual serving ramekins or one large soufflé dish, and again skim off the air bubbles.

Preheat the oven to 300°F. Place the ramekins in a pan of hot water and cover the pan tightly with foil. Bake for 55 to 60 minutes. Chill for at least 6 hours. When ready to serve, sprinkle each ramekin with the natural or brown sugar and broil for about 35 to 40 seconds.

MAKES 10 SERVINGS

White Chocolate Cheesecake

Although it is sinfully delectable, there is something virtuous-looking about this pure, creamy cheesecake.

Crust

2	cups graham cracker crumbs
⅓	cup blanched almonds, ground
¼	cup clarified butter

Filling

8	ounces white chocolate
4	(8-ounce) packages cream cheese, softened
½	cup plus 2 tablespoons sugar
4	large eggs plus 2 large egg yolks
2	tablespoons flour
1	teaspoon vanilla extract

For the crust, combine the crumbs, almonds, and butter. Press into the bottom and sides of a 10-inch springform pan.

For the filling, melt the chocolate in the top of a double boiler. Stir until smooth and remove from the heat. Beat the cream cheese with an electric mixer until fluffy and add the sugar. Beat in the eggs and egg yolks one at a time. Beat in the flour and vanilla; then add the melted chocolate in a slow, steady stream.

Preheat the oven to 250°F. Pour the mixture into the crust and bake for 1 hour or until firm.

MAKES 10 TO 12 SERVINGS

Lemon Squares

These are so good for a luncheon or afternoon tea.

1st layer

8   tablespoons (1 stick) butter

1½   cups confectioners' sugar

1½   cups all-purpose flour

2nd layer

2   eggs

1   cup granulated sugar

2   tablespoons all-purpose flour

2   tablespoons lemon juice

        Confectioners' sugar

Preheat the oven to 350°F.

For the first layer, combine the butter, sugar, and flour until crumbly then press into the bottom of a buttered 8 x 8-inch casserole. Bake for 20 minutes.

For the second layer, mix the eggs, granulated sugar, flour, and lemon juice in a bowl. Spread on top of the baked first layer. Bake at 350°F for another 20 minutes. Sprinkle with the confectioners' sugar.

MAKES 8 TO 12 SERVINGS

Rum Balls

Sissy credits her rum ball recipe to a friend, Michelle Harrington. "They make a terrific Christmas gift," she says, "if you can keep them around that long."

6	ounces chocolate chips
½	cup sugar plus sugar for rolling
⅓	cup Mt. Gay Rum (½ cup makes them really "juicy")
3	tablespoons light corn syrup
2	cups crushed vanilla wafers
1	cup ground walnuts

Melt the chips in the top of a double boiler. Remove from the heat. Stir in the sugar, rum, and syrup. Fold in the wafer crumbs and nuts. Shape into balls and roll them in the sugar. Store in an airtight container.

MAKES 12 TO 18 BALLS

Cider Sorbet with Red Wine Sauce

Here's a great dish to make in the autumn when apples and fresh-pressed cider are abundant. It is sweet, but the red wine sauce and crème fraîche add notes of sophistication that elevate it above the ice cream league.

Sorbet

2	cups cider
2	tablespoons lemon juice
¾	cup plus 1 tablespoon sugar
1	tablespoon vodka

Red Wine-Cinnamon Sauce

2	cups red wine
½	cup sugar
3	sticks cinnamon
	Dollop of crème fraîche or whipped cream

For the sorbet, combine the cider, lemon juice, sugar, and vodka in a mixing bowl. Stir until the sugar is dissolved. Refrigerate until thoroughly chilled, and pour the mixture into the container of an ice cream machine. Freeze following the manufacturer's instructions.

For the red wine-cinnamon sauce, combine the red wine, sugar, and cinnamon sticks in a saucepan and cook until reduced by half. Refrigerate until ready to use.

To serve, put a scoop of the cider sorbet in a sorbet dish. Top with the sauce and a dollop of crème fraîche or whipped cream.

MAKES 4 SERVINGS

Peach and Blueberry Cobbler

When blueberry season happens, it's glorious," says Sissy. "I get huge, succulent berries from Smokey House Project, a foundation that helps local children."

Cornmeal Topping

1 ¾	cups all-purpose flour
1	teaspoon baking soda
1	teaspoon baking powder
¼	teaspoon salt
¼	cup coarsely ground cornmeal
⅓	cup sugar
16	tablespoons (2 sticks) unsalted butter
1	teaspoon grated orange zest
1	egg
1	cup buttermilk

Filling

8	cups peeled and sliced fresh peaches
2	cups fresh blueberries
¼	teaspoon ground nutmeg
½	teaspoon vanilla extract
¾	cup sugar
1	tablespoon flour
¼	teaspoon ground cinnamon
1	tablespoon lemon juice

For the topping, sift together the flour, baking soda, baking powder, and salt. Add the cornmeal and sugar and mix well with your hands. Work in the butter until you have a coarse texture. Add the orange zest, egg, and buttermilk and work with you hands until you have a biscuit-like dough.

Preheat the oven to 350°F.

For the filling, combine the peaches, blueberries, nutmeg, vanilla, sugar, flour, cinnamon, and lemon juice in a large mixing bowl. Pour into a buttered 9 x 13-inch baking dish. Spread the topping evenly over the fruit to the edges of the pan. Bake for 45 to 50 minutes or until the topping is baked through.

MAKES 12 TO 14 SERVINGS

Bread Pudding

Infused with bourbon then dolloped with bourbon sauce, here is a bread pudding that you won't want to be serving to teetotaler friends. But for those who love the luxury of bread pudding and the woodsy smack of Kentucky bourbon, it's a large portion of heaven.

12	slices French baguette
2	tablespoons bourbon
4	plus 1 cups milk
2	cups half-and-half
1	cup sugar
6	whole eggs
4	egg yolks
1	teaspoon vanilla extract
1	teaspoon ground cinnamon
½	teaspoon ground nutmeg
1	cup raisins

Whiskey Sauce

16	tablespoons (2 sticks) butter
2	cups sugar
2	eggs
1	cup bourbon

Place the baguette slices in a large mixing bowl and soak with the bourbon and 1 cup milk. While the bread is soaking, heat the remaining 4 cups milk with the half-and-half in a medium-size pan over medium-high heat. Heat to the scalding stage. In a mixing bowl mix together the sugar, eggs, yolks, vanilla, cinnamon, and nutmeg. When the milk is scalded, whisk it into the egg mixture.

196

Preheat the oven to 350°F. Spread the raisins in a 9 x 13-inch baking pan. Lay the bread on top of the raisins. Pour the milk mixture over the bread. Press down with your hands to make sure the bread is totally soaked. Place the bread pudding pan in a water bath. Bake uncovered for about 1 hour or until firm in the middle and nicely browned on top. Remove from the oven and let cool.

For the whiskey sauce, melt the butter in a double boiler over low heat. While the butter is melting, mix together the sugar and the eggs in another bowl. Whisk the mixture into the melted butter. Stir until the sugar is dissolved and the eggs have thickened, about 5 minutes. Remove from the heat and cool to room temperature. Whisk in the bourbon. Serve the pudding with Whiskey Sauce.

MAKES 12 SERVINGS

My Mother's Pie Dough

Sissy notes that her mother's pie dough recipe makes enough for six 9-inch pie shells, and it will freeze well if you're not planning on making six pies at one time.

6	cups all-purpose flour
1	tablespoon sugar
1	tablespoon salt
1	pound lard
2	eggs
	Water

Mix the flour, sugar, and salt together in a medium-size mixing bowl. With your hands, work in the lard. Put the eggs into a one-cup measure and fill it with water. Add this to the flour and lard mixture. Mix just until it forms a dough. Do NOT overmix.

MAKES 6 PIECRUSTS

White Chocolate Brownies

While not at all fudgy, these luxurious squares will likely satisfy any hungry chocoholic.

14	*tablespoons butter*
8	*ounces white chocolate*
4	*eggs*
1	*cup sugar*
1	*tablespoon vanilla extract*
2	*cups all-purpose flour*
1	*cup white chocolate chips*
1	*cup semisweet chocolate chips*

Preheat the oven to 350°F. Melt the butter and white chocolate in the top of a double boiler over medium heat. Using the paddle attachment of an electric mixer, beat the eggs with the sugar at medium speed for about 5 minutes. Add the vanilla and then the melted chocolate mixture. Still using the paddle, add the flour and mix until it is fully incorporated. With the mixer still running, add the chocolate chips. Mix them in quickly and stop the machine. Scrape down the sides of the mixing bowl, and pour the mixture into a 9 x 13-inch, greased and floured, baking dish. Bake for 20 minutes or until a toothpick inserted in the center comes out clean.

MAKES 12 TO 14 SERVINGS

Blueberry Pie

There is no need to use the more precious wild Maine blueberries when making pie. In fact, we believe that regular, full-size berries have a more pie-worthy consistency as well as a surfeit of that unique indigo taste.

6	cups fresh or frozen blueberries
1	cup sugar
½	cup all-purpose flour
2	teaspoons lemon juice
1	teaspoon ground cinnamon
	Egg wash
2	piecrusts

Preheat the oven to 450°F. Mix together the blueberries, sugar, flour, lemon juice, and cinnamon in a bowl. Pour into the prepared pie shell. Brush the egg wash around the edges, place the second crust on top and crimp the edges. Brush the top with the remaining egg wash and cut small air slits in the top. Sprinkle with a little sugar. Bake in the oven for 15 minutes or until the crust starts to brown. Reduce the heat to 350°F and bake for about 40 minutes. The blueberries will begin to ooze out and the crust will be nicely browned.

MAKES 8 SERVINGS

Variation: For a crumb topping instead of the second piecrust, combine 8 tablespoons (1 stick) butter, ½ cup dark brown sugar, and 1 cup flour in a mixing bowl. Knead with your hands until the mix reaches the cornmeal stage, but is not clumpy. Spread the mixture over the pie and bake as above.

Streusel Cream Peach Pie

Peaches and cream are the soul of the tender filling in this crunch-topped pie.

1   unbaked pie shell, My Mother's Recipe (see page 197) or your choice

Filling

4   cups peeled and quartered peaches

½   cup sugar

½   teaspoon ground nutmeg

2   eggs, beaten

4   tablespoons cream

Topping

¼   cup brown sugar

½   cup all-purpose flour

4   tablespoons (½ stick) butter

Preheat the oven to 400°F.

For the filling, toss the peaches with the sugar, nutmeg, eggs, and cream. Pour into an unbaked pie shell.

For the topping, mix together the brown sugar and flour. Cut the butter into the mixture and sprinkle it evenly over the peaches. Bake for 15 minutes, turn the oven down to 350°F, and bake for another 40 minutes.

MAKES 8 SERVINGS

Coconut Cream Pie

We love the look of a coconut cream pie: all girlie-fluffy with the coconut shreds, and smooth and creamy, too.

1¼	cups milk
1¼	cups half-and-half
¾	cup sugar
½	cup all-purpose flour
	Pinch of salt
2	eggs
1	teaspoon vanilla extract
1½	plus ½ cups shredded coconut
1	piecrust (see page 197)
	Egg wash

Scald the milk and half-and-half. Whisk together the sugar, flour, salt, and eggs. Add the scalded milk mixture. Pour the batter into the top of a double boiler and whisk over medium heat until thick, about 15 minutes. Add the vanilla. Mix in the 1½ cups shredded coconut.

Preheat the oven to 350°F. While the pie mixture is cooling, roll out the piecrust. Lay it into a pie shell and cover with waxed paper. Fill the shell with navy beans (or any kind of bean that will weigh down the crust so it doesn't shrink during cooking). Bake in the oven until almost brown. Remove from the oven and remove the beans and paper. Brush the egg wash on the piecrust. Put the crust back in the oven for about 5 to 8 minutes or until cooked. Let the filling mixture cool and thicken. Pour it into the piecrust and chill. Toast the remaining ½ cup shredded coconut in the oven until just slightly brown. Sprinkle over the top of the pie.

MAKES 8 SERVINGS

Banana Cream Pie

We order banana cream pie every time we have the chance, and must admit that we are often disappointed. Ersatz pies are commonplace; and when you've had a really good one, like Sissy's recipe produces, such lame excuses for dessert will never satisfy.

1¼	cups milk
1¼	cups half-and-half
¾	cup sugar
½	cup all-purpose flour
	Pinch of salt
2	eggs
1	teaspoon vanilla extract
2	bananas
1	piecrust (see page 197)
	Egg wash

Scald the milk and half-and-half. Whisk together the sugar, flour, salt, and eggs. Add the scalded milk mixture. Pour the batter into the top of a double boiler and whisk over medium heat until thick, about 15 minutes. Add the vanilla.

Preheat the oven to 350°F. While the pie mixture is cooling, roll out the piecrust. Lay it into a pie shell and cover with waxed paper. Fill the shell with navy beans (or any kind of bean that will weigh down the crust so it doesn't shrink during cooking). Bake in the oven until almost brown. Remove from the oven and remove the beans and paper. Brush the egg wash on the piecrust. Put the crust back in the oven for about 5 to 8 minutes or until cooked. Let the filling mixture cool and thicken. Pour it into the piecrust and chill.

Pour one-third of the filling mixture into the piecrust. Slice 1 banana and layer the slices on the filling. Add another one-third of the filling, slice the second banana, and layer it on the pie. Top with the remaining one-third of the filling.

MAKES 8 SERVINGS

INDEX

Numbers in italics refer to pages with illustrations